SPOTLIGHT

FINGER LAKES

SASCHA ZUGER

Contents

FINGER LAKES

THE FINGER LAKES

It's hard to grasp the wealth of natural beauty, cornucopia of culinary delights, and unique cultural experiences to be had in this massive region, the equal to New Hampshire or New Jersey in size. At first glance, some might simply be attracted to tap into the tasting rooms, tempted to tread the stomping grounds of historical heroes, skim the surface of the glossy lakes, or sink under the mist of thundering waterfalls. It only takes one visit to realize the Finger Lakes is all of this and much more'and that you want to come back.

Fortunately, with the variety of sleepy villages and wild places to explore, this is one place where return trips are anything but replays of trips past. Much like the wine, the flavors here are rich and diverse and subtly change by the year.

According to Iroquois legend, the Finger Lakes were created when the Great Spirit reached out to bless the land and left imprints of his hands behind. Six of his fingers became the major Finger Lakes—Skaneateles, Owasco, Cayuga, Seneca, Keuka, and Canandaigua. The other four became the Little Finger Lakes—Honeoye, Canadice, Hemlock, and Conesus.

Geologists tell it differently. They say the long, skinny parallel lakes formed from the steady progressive grinding of at least two Ice Age glaciers. As the glaciers receded, the lake-valleys filled with rivers that were backed by dams of glacial debris.

The Finger Lakes are a singular place. Depending on the weather, the water varies in hue from a deep sapphire blue to a moody

© SASCHA ZUGER

HIGHLIGHTS

◖ **Skaneateles Village:** One of the prettiest of the Finger Lakes is anchored by a picturesque village of the same name, filled with cute shops and cafés (page 19).

◖ **Women's Rights National Historical Park:** The site of the first women's rights convention, organized by Elizabeth Cady Stanton and friends, met in the mill town of Seneca Falls in 1848. The park is complete with an informative visitors center and historic sites (page 28).

◖ **Mark Twain's Study:** Modeled after a Mississippi steamboat pilot house, the standalone octagonal study holds the iconic writer's typewriter, hat, pipe, and other belongings (page 45).

◖ **Harris Hill Soaring Center and National Soaring Museum:** Climb into a tiny engineless glider and soar over the Seneca Lake Valley with a pilot tailoring the flight to your tastes – from serene to exhilarating (page 47).

◖ **Corning Museum of Glass:** The state's third-most-popular tourist destination (after New York City and Niagara Falls) houses a remarkable collection of glass art spanning over 3,000 centuries, 40 daily interactive shows, and a studio where molten glass can be pulled into decorative shapes (page 49).

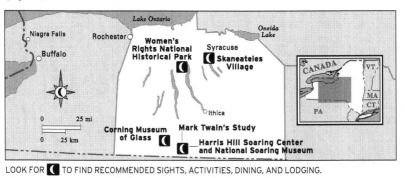

LOOK FOR ◖ TO FIND RECOMMENDED SIGHTS, ACTIVITIES, DINING, AND LODGING.

gray, while all around lie fertile farmlands heavy with fruit trees, buckwheat, and—especially—vineyards.

Along the lakes' southern edges, deep craggy gorges are sliced through the middle by silvery waterfalls. To the north preside hundreds of drumlins, or gentle glacier-created hills.

But scenic beauty tells only part of the Finger Lakes story. Despite its somnolent air, the region has an important industrial, civil rights, and religious history. In Auburn stand the homes of abolitionists Harriet Tubman and William Seward; Seneca Falls hosted the first Women's Rights Convention; and in Palmyra is the Sacred Grove where Joseph Smith, founder of the Mormon religion, is said to have first seen the Angel Moroni.

The region also holds a number of interesting small cities. Syracuse, the eastern gateway to the Finger Lakes, was once an Erie Canal boomtown. Ithaca, home to Cornell University, is surrounded by awesome steep gorges and waterfalls.

PLANNING YOUR TIME

The Finger Lakes is one of the largest regions in New York State, and to tour it all would take a good 10 days to two weeks. But it's also possible to see a substantial amount in three or four days, as traffic throughout the region is light and many of the most interesting sites are grouped together.

Most travelers will probably want to start their tour in **Skaneateles**, the prettiest of the Finger Lakes, which can easily be explored in an afternoon. Just down the road is **Auburn**, home to the fascinating house-museums of abolitionists William Seward and Harriet Tubman, and beyond that lies **Seneca Falls**, a must stop for anyone interested in women's history.

Outdoor lovers might want to focus on the southern side of the Finger Lakes region. Here, you'll find **Ithaca**, a university town surrounded by dramatic gorges and great hiking trails; the **Finger Lakes National Forest;** and, at the far western edge of the region, **Letchworth State Park**, home to the "Grand Canyon of the East."

Wine lovers should focus on **Hammondsport** and **Keuka Lake**, which have an especially large number of vineyards, as well as lovely scenic vistas. Culture buffs will want to spend two or three days in **Rochester.**

If you're traveling in July, be sure to find out the date of the **Hill Cumorah Pageant,** the Mormon celebration that commemorates the day when Joseph Smith received the Book of Mormon from the Angel Moroni. The largest, oldest, and most state-of-the-art outdoor drama in the United States, the pageant is well worth traveling out of your way to attend.

HISTORY
The People of the Longhouse
When French explorers first arrived in the Finger Lakes area in the early 1600s, they found it occupied by a confederacy of five Indian nations. The French called the Indians "Iroquois"; the Indians called themselves "Haudenosaunee," or "People of the Longhouse."

The Mohawk Nation (Keepers of the Eastern Door) lived to the east of what is considered the Finger Lakes region, along Schoharie Creek and the Mohawk River Valley. The Seneca (Keepers of the Western Door) lived to the west, along the Genesee River. In the middle were the Onondaga (Keepers of the Council Fire), and it was on

their territory the chiefs of the Five Nations met to establish policy and settle disputes. The two other "little brother" nations were the Cayuga, who resided between the Onondaga and the Seneca, and the Oneida, who lived between the Onondaga and the Mohawk. A sixth nation, the Tuscarora, joined the Iroquois confederacy in 1722.

During the Revolutionary War, all of the Iroquois except the Oneida sided with the British, as they had during the French and Indian War. Together with the Tories, they terrorized the pioneer villages and threatened the food supply of the Continental Army. In 1779, an angered General Washington sent Maj. Gen. John Sullivan into the region, ordering him to "lay waste all the settlements around so that the country may not only be overrun but destroyed." Sullivan punctiliously carried out his orders, annihilating 41 Iroquois settlements and burning countless fields and orchards. By the time he was done, the Iroquois nation was in ruins. Thousands fled to Canada; others were resettled onto reservations in 1784.

The Military Tract
After the Revolution, many of Sullivan's soldiers, impressed by the rich farmland they had seen, returned to the Finger Lakes, where they were given land in the "Military Tract" in lieu of payment. The tract, stretching roughly from Chittenango west to Geneva and from Ithaca north to Lake Ontario, covered some two million acres or one-sixteenth of present-day New York. The tract was divided into townships named by a surveyor with a love of the classics, hence the many Greek and Latin names remaining today: Ithaca, Ovid, Cato, Fabius, Manlius, Cicero, Dryden, Ulysses, Hector . . .

The region developed rapidly. Other settlers from New England and Pennsylvania arrived by the thousands, and by the early 1800s the woodlands of the Iroquois had become a busy agricultural region. Many communities sprang up on the sites of old Iroquois villages; many highways followed old Indian trails.

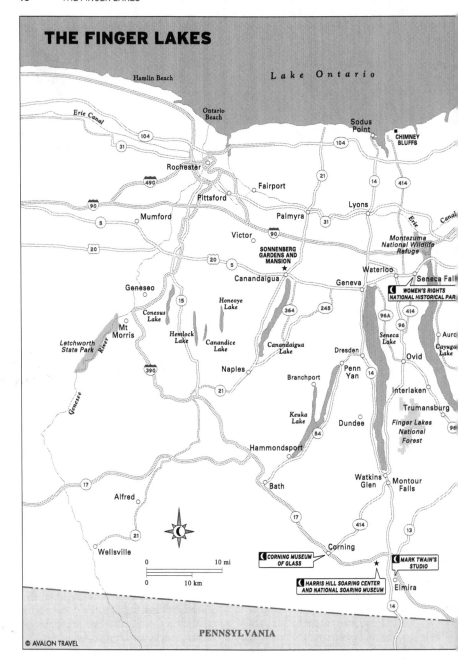

THE FINGER LAKES

Lake Ontario

Hamlin Beach

Ontario Beach

Sodus Point

CHIMNEY BLUFFS

Erie Canal

104

31

104

Rochester

Fairport

21

14

414

490

Lyons

Pittsford

Palmyra

31

Erie Canal

90

Mumford

Victor

90

Montezuma National Wildlife Refuge

5

SONNENBERG GARDENS AND MANSION

Waterloo

20

5

Canandaigua

Geneva

Seneca Fall

Geneseo

WOMEN'S RIGHTS NATIONAL HISTORICAL PAR

Honeoye Lake

15

364

245

96A

414

Conesus Lake

96

Mt Morris

Hemlock Lake

Canandice Lake

Canandaigua Lake

Seneca Lake

Aurc

Letchworth State Park

Dresden

Ovid

Cayuga Lake

390

Naples

Penn Yan

14

Interlaken

Branchport

Trumansburg

96

Keuka Lake

Dundee

Finger Lakes National Forest

21

Hammondsport

54

Watkins Glen

Montour Falls

Bath

Alfred

17

414

13

21

Corning

CORNING MUSEUM OF GLASS

MARK TWAIN'S STUDIO

Wellsville

0   10 mi

0   10 km

HARRIS HILL SOARING CENTER AND NATIONAL SOARING MUSEUM

Elmira

14

PENNSYLVANIA

© AVALON TRAVEL

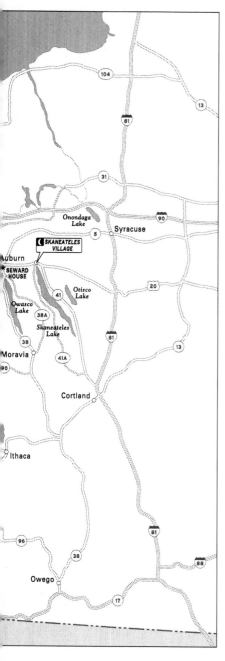

Prosperity and Reform

By 1825 the Erie Canal was completed, and the development of the Finger Lakes skyrocketed. Inland ports grew up all along the canal, and for 20 years, the area's rich farmland served as the breadbasket of the nation. When the Midwest took over that role, the Finger Lakes' farmers focused on fruit and dairy farming, shipping many of their goods east to New York City.

At the same time, the ports developed into major industrial centers. Extensive water power helped fuel the Industrial Revolution, and by the mid-1800s, factories manufacturing everything from woolens to glass flourished throughout the Finger Lakes. Syracuse, Auburn, Seneca Falls, and Elmira were among the largest manufacturing centers.

Along with increasing prosperity came increasing social unrest. Upstate New York in the late 1820s, '30s, and '40s was rocked by one fiery religious movement after another. Sects and cults sprang up all over the region until it became known as the "burned-over district." Among the best-known movements were the Perfectionists, led by John Humphrey Noyes in Oneida to the east; and the Mormons, founded by Joseph Smith in Palmyra. The religious fervor not only converted tens of thousands of citizens but also stimulated reform movements. Upstate became a hotbed for humanitarian causes, most notably the abolitionist and women's rights movements. Elizabeth Cady Stanton lived in Seneca Falls, Gerrit Smith in Peterboro and Skaneateles, and William Seward and later Harriet Tubman in Auburn. The first Women's Rights Convention convened in Seneca Falls in 1848, and one of the most dramatic rescues of a fugitive slave took place in Syracuse in 1851.

Modern Times

By the early 1900s, the dust settled. The Erie Canal declined in importance, thanks largely to the advent of the railroad; newer and larger factories opened up elsewhere; and the religious and reform movements lost fervor. The region's major cities remained important commercial centers, to be sure, but the rest of the land eased back into the sleepy agricultural state it is today.

GETTING THERE AND AROUND

The **Syracuse Hancock International Airport** is serviced by Jet Blue (800/JET-BLUE), American Airlines (800/433-7300), Continental (800/525-0280), Delta (800/221-1212), United (800/241-6522), and USAirways (800/428-4322). USAirways also services the **Tompkins County Airport** (Ithaca) and the **Elmira-Corning Regional Airport.** A taxi ride from any of these airports to their respective downtowns costs $14–20.

Amtrak (800/872-7245) travels to Syracuse. **Greyhound** (800/231-2222) and **New York State Trailways** (800/295-5555) provide bus service throughout the region.

By far the best way to explore the Finger Lakes is by car.

INFORMATION AND SERVICES

Walking tours are offered periodically by the **Landmark Society of Western New York** (585/546-7029, www.landmarksociety.org).

The **Finger Lakes Tourism Alliance** (309 Lake St., Penn Yan 14527, 315/536-7488 or 800/530-7488, www.fingerlakes.org) is a good central information source for the entire region.

Contact the **Finger Lakes Wine Country Tourism Marketing Association** (1 W. Market St., Corning 14830, 607/936-0706 or 800/813-2958, www.fingerlakeswinecountry.com) for information about the grape-growing regions around Keuka, Seneca, and Cayuga Lakes. Each of the lakes also has a "wine trail" website: www.keukawinetrail.com, www.senecawinetrail.com, and www.cayugawinetrail.com.

Several B&B registries operate in the Finger Lakes. Among them are the **Finger Lakes B&B Association** (877/422-6327, www.flbba.org), the **B&B Network of Central New York** (315/498-6560 or 800/333-1604, www.cnylodging.com), and the **B&B Association of**

Greater Ithaca (607/589-6073 or 800/806-4406, www.bbithaca.com).

Many counties, cities, and towns also have their own visitor information centers, listed below. Most are open 9 A.M.–5 P.M. Monday–Friday.

- **Greater Syracuse/Onondaga County Convention and Visitors Bureau:** 572 S. Salina St., Syracuse 13202, 315/470-1910 or 800/234-4797, www.visitsyracuse.org

- **Skaneateles Chamber of Commerce:** 22 Jordan St., Skaneateles 13152, 315/685-0552, www.skaneateles.com

- **Cayuga County Office of Tourism:** 131 Genesee Street, Auburn 13021, 315/255-1658 or 800/499-9615, www.cayugacountychamber.com

- **Seneca County Tourism:** 1 DiPronio Dr., Waterloo 13165, 315/539-1759 or 800/732-1848, www.visitsenecany.net

- **Ithaca/Tompkins County Convention and Visitors Bureau:** 904 East Shore Dr., Ithaca 14850, 607/272-1313 or 800/284-8422, www.visitithaca.com

- **Geneva Area Chamber of Commerce:** 35 Lakefront Dr., Geneva, 315/789-1776 or 877/5-GENEVA, www.genevany.com

- **Chemung County Chamber of Commerce:** 400 E. Church St., Elmira 14901, 607/734-5137 or 800/627-5892, www.chemungchamber.org

- **Corning–Steuben County Conference & Visitors Bureau** 1 W. Market St., Corning 14830, 607/936-6544 or 1-866-WINE-FUN, www.corningfingerlakes.com

- **Canandaigua-Finger Lakes Visitors Connection:** 25 Gorham St., Canandaigua 14424, 585/394-3915, www.visitfingerlakes.com

- **Wayne County Tourism:** 9 Pearl St., Suite 3, Lyons, 14489, 800/527-6510, www.waynecountytourism.com

Syracuse

The main streets of Syracuse are oddly wide and flat, fat gray rubber bands stretched out to their sides. It begs the question: who would lay out a city with so much empty space? The answer is simple. One street was once the Erie Canal (Erie Boulevard); another, the Genesee Valley Turnpike (Genesee Street).

Like many towns in central New York, Syracuse boomed with the opening of the Erie Canal. But long before the canal, settlers were attracted to the area by its many valuable salt springs. As early as 1797, the state took over the springs in order to obtain tax revenues on salt, then worth so much it was referred to as "white gold."

With the opening of the Erie Canal, the salt industry developed rapidly, reaching a high point of eight million bushels a year during the Civil War. Other Syracuse industries flourished as well, including foundries and machine shops. The Irish, who had arrived to dig the canal, remained to work the factories and were soon joined by large numbers of German immigrants.

After the Civil War, other industries took over: among them, typewriters, ceramics, and Franklin cars, equipped with air-cooled engines. The Irish and Germans were joined by Italians, Poles, Russians, Ukrainians, and African Americans.

Today, Syracuse still supports a wide variety of peoples and industries, including the Niagara Mohawk Power Corporation, Bristol-Myers Squibb, and Syracuse University. The fourth-largest city in the state (pop. 140,000), Syracuse also has its share of urban ills.

Orientation

The heart of Syracuse is Clinton Square, where Erie Boulevard and Genesee Street meet. The main business district lies just south of the square and is dominated by Salina and Montgomery Streets. Syracuse University sits on a hill to the southeast, while to the northwest is Onondaga Lake. South of the city, the sovereign 7,300-acre Onondaga Reservation houses about 750 Native Americans. The Iroquois Confederacy's Grand Council of Chiefs still meets here every year, as it has for centuries.

I-90 runs east-west north of downtown. I-81 runs north-south through the center of the city. Street parking is generally available. Sights downtown are within easy walking distance of each other.

DOWNTOWN SIGHTS
Heritage Area Visitor Center and Erie Canal Museum

This long, low-slung 1850s building (318 Erie Blvd., at Montgomery St., 315/471-0593, www.eriecanalmuseum.org, 10 A.M.–5 P.M. Mon.–Sat., 10 A.M.–3 P.M. Sun., free admission) was once an Erie Canal weigh station for boats. Today, it's home to a visitors center, historical exhibits, a theater where a good introductory film on the city is screened, and a 65-foot-long reconstructed canal boat. In the boat remain the original personal effects of some early passengers, including one heartbreaking letter from an Irishwoman who had just buried her husband at sea.

Syracuse is one of New York's Heritage Areas—loosely delineated historic districts linked by a common theme. The Syracuse theme is transportation, and business and capital. Free walking-tour brochures can be picked up here.

West on Erie Boulevard

Heading west two blocks from the visitors center, you'll reach the heart of the city, **Clinton Square.** The former intersection of the Erie Canal and Genesee Valley Turnpike, the square in days past teemed with farmers' wagons, peddlers' carts, canal boats, hawkers, musicians, and organ grinders. Today, many free outdoor events are held here.

In the mid-1800s, Clinton Square evolved from a marketplace into a financial center. The four bank buildings along Salina Street—all on the National Register of Historic Places—hark

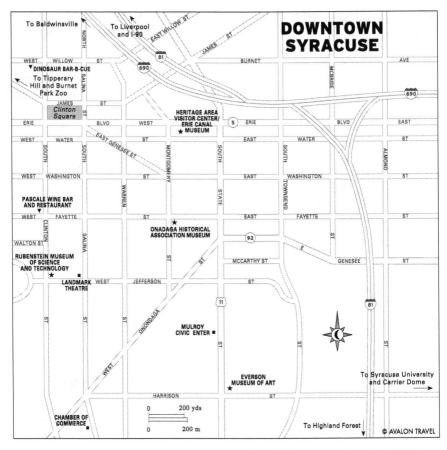

To Baldwinsville
To Liverpool and I-90

DOWNTOWN SYRACUSE

WEST WILLOW ST
DINOSAUR BAR-B-CUE
To Tipperary Hill and Burnet Park Zoo
JAMES ST
Clinton Square
ERIE BLVD WEST
HERITAGE AREA VISITOR CENTER/ ERIE CANAL ★ MUSEUM
ERIE BLVD EAST
WEST WATER ST
EAST WATER ST
WEST WASHINGTON ST
EAST WASHINGTON ST
PASCALE WINE BAR AND RESTAURANT
WEST FAYETTE ST
EAST FAYETTE ST
ONANDAGA HISTORICAL ASSOCIATION MUSEUM
WALTON ST
RUBENSTEIN MUSEUM OF SCIENCE AND TECHNOLOGY
MCCARTHY ST
GENESEE ST
LANDMARK THEATRE WEST JEFFERSON
MULROY CIVIC ENTER
To Syracuse University and Carrier Dome
EVERSON MUSEUM OF ART
HARRISON ST
0 200 yds
0 200 m
CHAMBER OF COMMERCE
To Highland Forest
© AVALON TRAVEL

back to those days. The four-sided, 100-foot clock tower on the 1867 Gridley Building was originally lit by gas jets.

At the western end of Clinton Square, near Clinton Street, stands the **Jerry Rescue Monument.** The monument commemorates William "Jerry" McHenry, born into slavery in North Carolina around 1812. Jerry successfully escaped to Syracuse, where he got a job in a cooper's shop making salt barrels. There he was discovered and arrested by federal marshals in 1851. A vigilante abolitionist group headed by Gerrit Smith and Dr. Samuel J. May attacked the police station and rescued Jerry, who fled to Canada a few days later. That rescue, which

challenged the Fugitive Slave Act of 1850, was one of the early precipitating events leading up to the Civil War.

One block further west on Erie Boulevard at Franklin Street reigns the stunning **Niagara Mohawk Power Corporation** building. Completed in 1932, the steel-and-black structure is a superb example of art deco architecture. The edifice is especially worth seeing at night, when it's lit by colored lights.

Armory Square District

Head south on Franklin Street three blocks, and you'll find yourself in the redbrick Armory Square District, Syracuse's answer to

THE VINEYARDS OF THE FINGER LAKES

The hills of the Finger Lakes, covered with vineyards, glow pale green in spring, dust green in summer, red-brown-purple in fall. Ideal grape-growing conditions came about tens of thousands of years ago when the retreating glaciers deposited a layer of topsoil on shale beds above the lakes. The lakes in turn create a microclimate that moderates the region's temperatures.

In 1829 near Hammondsport, a Reverend Bostwick planted a few grapevines to make sacramental wine. His successful efforts were duly noted by his neighbors, and soon vineyards ringed the village. In 1860, 13 Hammondsport businesspeople banded together to form the country's first commercial winery – the Pleasant Valley Wine Company – and dozens of other entrepreneurs soon followed suit.

For many years, the Finger Lakes vineyards produced only native American Concord, Delaware, and Niagara grapes, used in the production of ho-hum sweet and table wines. About 25 years ago, however, several viticulturists began experimenting with the more complex European Vinifera grape, and today, excellent chardonnays, Rieslings, seyval blancs, and sparkling wines are made throughout the region.

The Finger Lakes currently boasts close to 50 wineries, most hugging the shores of Cayuga, Seneca, or Keuka Lakes. Each lake has its own wine-growing association that publishes its own free maps and brochures, available throughout the region.

Most wineries are open May-October, 10 A.M.-5 P.M. Monday-Saturday and noon-5 P.M. Sunday, with more limited hours off-season. Tastings are usually free, but sometimes cost $1-2.

Some of the region's best wineries are described by geographic location throughout this chapter. For a complete list, contact the **New York Wine and Grape Foundation** (315/536-7442, www.newyorkwines.org).

Greenwich Village. At one end hulks the old Syracuse Armory, while all around are shops, cafés, and restaurants. The district centers on the junction of Franklin and Walton Streets.

Rubenstein Museum of Science and Technology

The old Syracuse Armory now houses the MOST, a.k.a. the Rubenstein Museum of Science and Technology (500 S. Franklin St., at W. Jefferson St., 315/425-9068, www.most.org, 10 A.M.-5 P.M. Wed.-Sun., adults $5, seniors and children 2-11 $4). The MOST moved into this location in 1992. The armory's former Riding Hall now holds exhibits on the earth, the human body, and the environment; the former Drill Hall showcases a 225-seat IMAX theater (tickets $9). Especially popular with kids are the old 1863 stables, now packed with hands-on exhibits, and the Silverman Planetarium.

Landmark Theatre

Just 1.5 blocks east of the MOST stands the 2,922-seat Landmark Theatre (362 S. Salina St., at E. Jefferson St., 315/475-7979, www.landmarktheatre.org, 10 A.M.-5 P.M. Mon.-Fri., tours by appointment), designed in 1928 by Thomas Lamb, a preeminent movie-palace architect. The building's relatively sedate exterior does little to prepare you for its riotous interior—an ornate Indo-Persian fantasy bestrewn with gold carvings. Nearly destroyed by a wrecking ball in the 1970s, the Landmark is now a beloved local institution.

Onondaga Historical Association Museum

One of the best county museums in the state, this fine institution (321 Montgomery St., between E. Jefferson and Fayette Sts., 315/428-1864, www.cnyhistory.org, 10 A.M.-4 P.M. Wed.-Fri., 11 A.M.-4 P.M. Sat.-Sun., free admission) covers virtually every aspect of Central New York's history, from the Onondaga Nation and early African American settlers to the Erie Canal and the salt industry. One display explores the 50 breweries that once operated in Syracuse; another, the city's natural history. A plethora of historic maps, photographs, paintings, and artifacts are displayed.

Everson Museum of Art

Housed in a sleek 1968 building designed by I. M. Pei, the Everson (401 Harrison St., at State St., 315/474-6064, www.everson.org, noon–5 P.M. Tues.–Fri. and Sun., 10 A.M.–5 P.M. Sat., free admission) contains one of the world's largest collections of ceramics. The museum also displays small but fine collections of 18th-century American portraits, African and Latin American folk art, and contemporary photography. Temporary exhibits usually focus on one major American artist such as Winslow Homer, Ansel Adams, or Helen Frankenthaler.

SIGHTS AROUND TOWN
Rosamond Gifford Zoo at Burnet Park

The 36-acre Rosamond Gifford Zoo (500 Burnet Park Dr., off S. Wilbur Ave., 315/435-8511, http://rosamondgiffordzoo.org, 10 A.M.–4:30 P.M. daily, adults $6.50; seniors and students $4.50, and children 3–15 $4) on the west side of town houses close to 1,000 animals and birds living in re-created natural habitats. The various inhabitants enjoy an arctic tundra, a tropical rain forest, an arid desert, and a region called the Wild North. A successful Humboldt penguin breeding program (the zoo recently welcomed its thirteenth chick), Adaptation of Animals exhibit, public overnights, and meet-the-elephant opportunities are a few of the zoo's highlights.

Tipperary Hill

Also west of downtown, at the juncture of West Fayette and West Genesee Streets, is the "Gateway to Tipperary Hill." Syracuse's oldest Irish neighborhood, Tipperary Hill is known for its **upside-down traffic light** at the intersection of Tompkins and Lowell Streets—the only one in the country. When the stoplight was first installed, right-side-up, its lenses were immediately destroyed by irate citizens who did not want British red placed above Irish green.

The city's fathers, realizing this was one battle they could never win, reversed the lenses to accommodate the neighborhood.

In the heart of today's Tipperary Hill, now only about half Irish, stands the **Cashel House** (224 Tompkins St., 315/472-4438), packed with goods imported from Ireland. Across the street, **Coleman's Authentic Irish Pub** (100 S. Lowell Ave., 315/476-1933) boasts both human- and leprechaun-size doors, along with Irish pub grub.

Salt Museum

To the north, in the suburb of Liverpool, lies lozenge-shaped Onondaga Lake, whose rich salt deposits first attracted settlers to the area. Unfortunately, the lake is now seriously polluted, but to one side stands a homespun museum (Onondaga Lake Pkwy./Rte. 370, 315/453-6715 or 315/453-6767, 1–6 P.M. daily May–Sept., free admission) equipped with an original "boiling block." Brine was once turned into salt here through boiling and solar evaporation. On display are battered antique iron kettles, wooden barrels, and other equipment, along with a fascinating collection of historic photographs.

The museum and lake belong to **Onondaga Lake Park,** which also offers bicycle rentals, a tram ride, a playground, and Ste. Marie Among the Iroquois—a second museum on the other side of the parkway.

Ste. Marie Among the Iroquois

Much more elaborate than the Salt Museum, Ste. Marie Among the Iroquois (Onondaga Lake Pkwy./Rte. 370, 315/453-6767, interpretive guides on site noon–5 P.M. Sat.–Sun., self-guided tours 9 A.M.–3 P.M., Mon.–Fri., May–Oct., adults $3, seniors $2.50, children ages 6–17 $2) re-creates the 17th-century world of the French Jesuits and Iroquois who once lived on the shores of Onondaga Lake. The exhibit begins indoors with displays on the Onondaga, then explores the meeting between the two cultures through artifacts, art, and historical documents.

Outdoors in a re-created French fort,

costumed guides forge horseshoes, bake bread, and hollow out canoes. The French only lived in the area for 20 months. The Onondaga welcomed their presence, but the Mohawk did not, and in March 1658 the French withdrew. Their legacy lives on in the large community of Catholic Onondagas residing in Syracuse today.

Owned by the county, the Ste. Marie museum was shut down in 2002, due to a lack of funding, but concerned citizens, who hated to see the beautiful site fall into ruin, started it up again. Today, Ste. Marie is largely volunteer-run.

ENTERTAINMENT AND EVENTS
Performing Arts
One of the more unusual arts organizations in town is the **Open Hand Theater** (518 Prospect Ave., 315/476-0466, www.openhandtheater.org), featuring giant puppets from around the world. Connected to the theater is an **International Mask and Puppet Museum** (518 Prospect Ave., 315/476-0466, www.openhandtheater.org, Fri. by appointment and performance Sat.), complete with hands-on activities.

The **Syracuse Symphony Orchestra** (411 Montgomery St., 315/424-8222, Oct.–May) performs classical and popular music concerts at John H. Mulroy Civic Center. The **Landmark Theatre** (362 S. Salina St., 315/475-7979) hosts concerts, plays, dance troupes, and classic movies throughout the year.

Nightlife
The best source for what's going on where is the *Syracuse New Times* (315/422-7011), a free alternative newsweekly available throughout the city. Many bars and clubs are located in the **Armory Square District** (www.armorysquare.com).

One of the liveliest music clubs in town is **Dinosaur Bar-B-Cue** (246 W. Willow St., 315/476-4937), a friendly hole-in-the-wall filled with dinosaurs and blues paraphernalia, bikers and businesspeople. Live blues is performed most nights.

A good club in which to hear local bands is **Shifty's** (1401 Burnet Ave., 315/474-0048). On weekends, traditional Irish music fills the **Limerick Pub** (134 Walton St., 315/475-1819).

Events
The **Syracuse Jazz Fest** (http://syracusejazzfest.com) is the largest free jazz festival in the Northeast. The celebration runs for seven days in mid-June, and features a wide variety of jazz events, artists, and styles. In July, the city hosts a smaller but growing **Blues Festival** (www.nysbluesfest.com). In July and August, the Syracuse Pops and the Syracuse Orchestra play **free concerts** (315/470-1910) in the city's parks.

One of the state's grandest parties is the **New York State Fair** (New York State Fairgrounds, 581 State Fair Blvd., Exit 7 off I-690, www.nystatefair.org, 315/487-7711), featuring agricultural and livestock competitions, music and entertainment, amusement rides and games of chance, business and industrial exhibits, and talent competitions. The fair runs for 12 days, ending on Labor Day, and attracts about 850,000 people.

In November, the **Festival of Nations** (315/470-1910) celebrates the traditions, song, and dance of 35 Native American groups.

SPORTS AND RECREATION
Mid-Lakes Navigation (315/685-8500 or 800/545-4318, www.midlakesnav.com) offers excursion and dinner cruises on the Erie Canal. The boats leave from Dutchman's Landing off Route 370 north of Liverpool. The company also offers three-day cruises and has boats available for weekly rental.

Take in a Syracuse University football, basketball, or lacrosse game at the 50,000-seat **Carrier Dome** (900 Irving Ave., 315/443-4634).

ACCOMMODATIONS
In a lovely residential neighborhood just east of downtown stands the ❰ **Dickerson House on James** (1504 James St., 315/423-4777, www.dickersonhouse.com, $99–350 d). This stately English Tudor B&B offers five attractive

guest rooms filled with antiques, a small garden out back, and a guest kitchen generously stocked with snacks, beer, and wine.

In Fayetteville, 10 miles southeast of Syracuse, find the comfortable **Craftsman Inn** (7300 E. Genesee St., 315/637-8000, www.craftsmaninn.com, $99–180), where all 90-odd rooms and suites are furnished in Arts and Crafts style.

The downtown **Parkview Hotel** (713 E. Genesee St., 315/701-2600, www.theparkviewhotel.com, $97–109) is a charming boutique hotel with large, art deco–styled rooms and a good, solid coffee bar in Stefon's Place, which serves light meals on the first floor. Complimentary airport shuttle and Wi-Fi add to the already decent value.

C Jefferson Clinton Hotel (416 S. Clinton St, 315/425-0500, www.jeffersonclintonhotel.com, $195–300) with warm, genuine service, impresses guests with the little touches, from the rubber ducky atop the generous stack of bath towels to an omelet station at the complimentary breakfast buffet. Complimentary Wii, X-Box 360, DVD and GPS rentals, Wi-Fi, and parking are added perks. What might be most winning, though, is the hotel's habit of scooting guests to their room on early arrivals whenever humanly possible and their practice of free upgrades to available junior suites. The Armory Square location offers easy access to pubs, museums, and the large ice-skating pavilion in the winter.

FOOD

In the Armory Square District, try **Pastabilities** (311 S. Franklin St., 315/474-1153, $11) for home-cooked Italian fare. Significantly more upscale is **C Pascale Wine Bar & Restaurant** (204 W. Fayette St., 315/471-3040, $17), a historic townhouse serving imaginative French-American cuisine and Finger Lakes wines. Also in the neighborhood, the **Lemon Grass Grille and 238 Bistro** (238 W. Jefferson St., 315/475-1111, $15) specializes in Pacific Rim cuisine.

C Dinosaur Bar-B-Cue (246 W. Willow St., 315/476-4937), known statewide for their winning sauces, is awhirl with murals of frolicking dinosaurs and a row of Harley's frequently parked out front, which business folk on their lunch breaks slip past to get their sauce on. The fun, bustling hotspot serves straightforward barbecue dishes and home-style comfort foods for lunch and dinner; fried green tomatoes and pulled pork sandwiches are two favorites. The blues club brings in top acts for live music, served with a side of mac 'n cheese.

C The Mission Restaurant (304 E. Onondaga St., 315/475-7344, $14) is built to look like a tiny church, complete with a steeple and stained-glass windows. On the menu is Mexican and Caribbean fare, along with great margaritas.

Clam Bar (3914 Brewerton Rd., 315/458-1662, $14), with a deceptively 1950s kitsch dive-ish look, complete with knotty pine walls and motorcycle parking, fronts a family-owned place touted for the best seafood in town. This claim is backed up by the crowd, which you'll want to get there early to avoid.

In Tipperary Hill, **Coleman's Authentic Irish Pub** (100 S. Lowell Ave., 315/476-1933) is a neighborhood institution featuring menus written in both Gaelic and English, and lots of hearty Irish fare. For Old World German food in a simple setting, try **Weber's Grill** (820 Danforth St., 315/472-0480), also a Syracuse institution, located north of downtown.

EXCURSIONS FROM SYRACUSE

Beaver Lake Nature Center

This serene 560-acre nature preserve (8477 East Mud Lake Rd., off Rte. 370, Baldwinsville, 315/638-2519, 7:30 A.M.–dusk daily, $3 per car) 18 miles northwest of Syracuse offers 10 miles of well-marked trails and boardwalks, along with a 200-acre lake that's a favorite resting spot for migrating duck and geese. A visitors center displays exhibits on local flora and fauna.

Highland Forest

Onondaga County's largest and oldest park is the 2,700-acre Highland Forest (off Rte. 80, 315/683-5550, dawn–dusk daily, free admission), in Fabius, about a 30-minute drive southeast of Syracuse. Spread out atop Arab Hill, the park offers great views of the surrounding countryside.

Adirondack-like in appearance, the forest is laced with four hiking trails ranging in length from less than a mile to eight miles. One-hour guided trail rides on horseback are offered April–November, while hay and sleigh rides are offered on fall and winter weekends.

Green Lakes State Park

About 10 miles due east of Syracuse, the 2,000-acre Green Lakes State Park (7900 Green Lakes Rd., off Rte. 290, Fayetteville, 315/637-6111, dawn–dusk daily, $6–8 parking) contains two aquamarine glacial lakes. Facilities include a swimming beach, hiking and biking trails, playground, campground, and 18-hole golf course. Boats can also be rented. For campground reservations, call 800/456-CAMP.

Skaneateles Lake Area

The farthest east of the Finger Lakes, deep blue Skaneateles (Scan-ee-AT-i-less) is also the highest (867 feet above sea level) and most beautiful. Fifteen miles long and 1–2 miles wide, the lake is surrounded by gentle rolling hills to the south and more majestic, near-mountainous ones to the north. Iroquois for "long lake," Skaneateles is spring fed, crystal clean, and clear. In the summer, its waters are specked with sailboats; in the winter, ice fishers build igloos.

The only real village on the lake is Skaneateles. Elsewhere along the shoreline preside handsome summer homes placed judicious distances apart.

SKANEATELES

The charming village of Skaneateles spreads out along one long main street (Route 20) at the north end of the lake. Graceful 19th-century homes, white-columned public buildings, and trim brick storefronts are everywhere and make for excellent strolling surrounds. Skaneateles has been a favorite retreat among wealthy Syracusans for generations.

The first Europeans in Skaneateles were Moravian missionaries who visited an Onondaga village here in 1750. From 1843 to 1845, the village was the short-lived site of a Utopian community that advertised in the newspapers for followers and advocated communal property, nonviolence, easy divorce, and vegetarianism. Prior to the Civil War,

Skaneateles served as the headquarters for abolitionist Gerrit Smith and was an important stop on the Underground Railroad.

◖ Skaneateles Village

In the center of the village is **Clift Park,** a waterfront refuge with a gazebo and wide-angled views of the lake. Docked at the end of a small pier are the two classic wooden boats of the **Mid-Lakes Navigation Co.** (315/685-8500 or 800/545-4318, www.midlakes-nav.com, May–Sept.). During the warmer months, the family-owned spit-and-polish vessels offer enjoyable sightseeing, lunch, and dinner cruises. These same craft also deliver the mail on Skaneateles Lake—a 100-plus-year-old tradition. The knowledgeable captain offers insight into the passing sights and properties, some of which her family settled generations before.

Across from the park stands the hospitable **Sherwood Inn** (26 W. Genesee St., 315/685-3405, www.thesherwoodinn.com) a rambling, Colonial blue building that was once a stagecoach stop. The inn was established in 1807 by one Isaac Sherwood, a man who began his career by delivering the mail on foot between Utica and Canandaigua, and ended it as the "stagecoach king."

Just down the street is **Krebs** (53 W. Genesee St., 315/685-5714), a Finger Lakes institution dating back to 1899. For many years, Krebs reigned as the best restaurant in New York

ENJOYING THE DICKENS OUT OF THE FINGER LAKES

Touting the entrance to its holiday festival as the "world's smallest Christmas parade," the picturesque village of Skaneateles welcomes Scrooge, Bob Cratchit, Tiny Tim, and other favorite characters to stroll down the main drag to the grand opening of the impressive **Dickens Christmas in Skaneateles** (www. skaneateles.com, running weekends from the day after Thanksgiving until Christmas) on the steps of the Sherwood Inn.

There are free horse and carriage rides, free roasted chestnuts, and free hot cider and donuts (or hot chocolate served by village Girl Scouts). There's also caroling on most every street corner, a sing-along in the village gazebo, Mother Goose storytime, and Father Christmas giving out free treats for the best little visitors. Live Dickens characters interact with townsfolk and visitors in the shops and along the streets and perform scenes from *A Christmas Carol*. With all this, it's safe to say this 16-year-old holiday tradition is looking forward to a long future of celebrating the old-fashioned way.

outside Manhattan, and diners flocked here from all over the state. At its peak in 1920, Krebs served 3,000 meals a day.

A great place for an espresso stop or leisurely browse over a glass of wine is the independent bookshop and cafe **Creekside Books and Coffee** (35 Fennell St. 315/685-0379 www.creeksidecoffeehouse.com) which offers wine tastings, author readings, cooking demos and live music in a cozy, bookish atmosphere.

The Creamery

To learn about the lake's history, step into this small local museum (28 Hannum St., 315/685-1360, 1–4 P.M. Fri. year-round, 1–4 P.M. Thurs.–Sat. May–Sept., free admission) housed in the former Skaneateles Creamery building. From 1899 to 1949, area farmers brought their milk here to be turned into buttermilk, cream, and butter. Displays include scale models of the boats that once sailed the lake, exhibits on dairy farming, and information about the teasel, a thistle-like plant once used in woolen mills to raise a cloth's nap. For 120 years, Skaneateles was the teasel-growing capital of the United States. The Creamery is run by the **Skaneateles Historical Society** (28 Hannum St., 315/685-1360, www.skaneateleshistoricalsociety.org), which also offers walking tours of the village.

New Hope Mills

For spectacular views of the lake, drive down either Route 41 to the east or Route 41A to the west. Route 41A veers away from the shoreline at the southern end and leads to New Hope Mills (181 York Street, Auburn, 315/497-0783, 9 A.M.–5 P.M. Mon.–Fri. and 10 A.M.–2 P.M. Sat. May–Dec.), an 1823 flour mill where grain is still ground with granite and burr stones operated by a 26-foot overshot waterwheel. Unbleached flours and grains are for sale.

Events

As you might expect, all the big events take place in the summer months. Weekly **sailboat races** (2745 East Lake Rd., www.skansailclub.com, 5:30 P.M. Wed., 2 P.M. Sat.–Sun, Jun.–Aug.) take place throughout the summer, while free **band concerts** (West Genesee Street, across from the Sherwood Inn, www.skaneateles.com, 7:30 P.M. in July, 7 P.M. in Aug.)are held on Friday evenings in Clift Park. **Polo games** are played on Sunday afternoons in July and August at the Skaneateles Polo Club (West Lake and Andrews Rds.). Since 1980, the **Skaneateles Festival** (www.skanfest.org) has been bringing top chamber-music artists to town in August. The town's largest event is the **antique and classic boat show** (north end of Lake Skaneateles, 315/685-0552, www.skaneateles.com)in early July.

participants in the Dickens Christmas in Skaneateles festival

Accommodations

The upscale yet casual **(Sherwood Inn** (26 W. Genesee St., 315/685-3405, www.thesherwoodinn.com, $95–195 d) includes a very popular restaurant, a tavern with frequent live entertainment, and 24 attractive guest rooms, all decorated with antiques. Contributing to the inn's relaxed atmosphere are a big screened-in porch with wonderful views of the lake, an outdoor patio for summer dining, lots of fresh flowers, and a snug lounge.

Near the heart of downtown is **The Gray House** (47 Jordan St., 315/685-0131, $89–150 d), a welcoming B&B housed in a spacious Victorian home, complete with four guest rooms, a large parlor, two breezy porches, and gardens.

Hobbit Hollow Farm (3061 West Lake Rd., 315/685-2791, www.hobbithollow.com, $100–170), a century-old Colonial Revival farmhouse overlooks Lake Skaneateles from a picturesque perch of 400 acres. This four-season property offers a full country breakfast, afternoon wine and cheese tasting, Wi-Fi, spa robes, snowshoes, and private baths.

On the outskirts of Skaneateles is the ultra-luxurious **Mirbeau Inn and Spa** (851 W. Genesee St., 315/685-5006 or 877/647-2328, www.mirbeau.com, $185–385 d). An elegant, European-style inn complete with wall frescoes, waterfalls, soft lighting, and 34 spacious guest rooms, the Mirbeau offers a wide variety of spa treatments. The inn is also known for its serene restaurant.

Food

One of the oldest restaurants in the Finger Lakes (Franklin Roosevelt and Charles Lindbergh once ate here), **(Krebs** (53 W. Genesee St., 315/685-5714, open May–Oct. for dinner only), is most famous for its seven-course continental dinners ($44 per person), but also serves lighter fare. Three basic entrés are served—chicken, lobster, and prime rib—along with homemade soups and baked goods. Out back is a formal garden while upstairs is a low-ceilinged tavern where locals congregate.

The laid-back **(Doug's Fish Fry** (8 Jordan St., 315/685-3288) is a local favorite, renowned for its chowder, fried scallops, gumbo, and fish sandwiches.

Rosalie's Cucina (841 W. Genesee St., 315/685-2200, $17) offers first-rate Italian fare, ranging from pizza and pasta to grilled lobster tails, in an adobe taverna. For fresh Japanese food in a peaceful setting, step into **Kabuki** (12 W. Genesee St., 315/685-7234, $8–20).

In addition to great accommodations, the Sherwood Inn and Mirbeau Inn are also excellent dining choices. The restaurant at the **Mirbeau** (851 W. Genesee St., 315/685-5006 or 877/647-2328, www.mirbeau.com) serves creative American cuisine that uses fresh local ingredients. The menu often changes daily; four- and five-course prix fixe dinners cost $49–54. The restaurant at the **Sherwood Inn** (26 W. Genesee St., 315/685-3405, www.thesherwoodinn.com, $15) features traditional American fare. Check out the **Patisserie** (4 Hannum St., 315/685-2433) which provides all the breads for the Sherwood Inn, a perfect stop for a great morning coffee and pastry.

CORTLAND

About 12 miles from the southern tip of Skaneateles Lake sprawls the city of Cortland (pop. 19,800). Set in the midst of fertile farm country, Cortland was once a small industrial center, best known for its wire cloth, lingerie, and corset factories. Along Main Street between Tompkins Street and Clinton Avenue is a **National Historic District** of handsome homes and commercial buildings.

Cortland also claims literary fame. It was here that Chester Gillette, the real-life counterpart to the character Clyde Griffiths in Theodore Dreiser's *An American Tragedy,* met Grace Brown. Writes Dreiser of Griffiths' arrival in his new hometown: "He found himself ambling on and on until suddenly he was…in touch with a wide and tree-shaded thoroughfare of residences, the houses of which, each and every one, appeared to possess more room space, lawn space, general ease and repose and dignity even than any with which he had ever been in contact. . . ." Gillette once worked in his uncle's Gillette Skirt Factory on the north

side of town, and lived in the still-standing double house at No. 17 East Main Street.

1890 House Museum

Perhaps one of the houses spotted by Gillette/ Griffiths in his ramble was the castlelike 1890 House Museum (37 Tompkins St./Rte. 13, 607/756-7551, www.1890house.org, 1–4 P.M. Thurs.–Sat. year-round, adults $5, seniors and students $3, children under 12 free), built by wire manufacturer Chester F. Wickwire. Now an informal museum, the house holds 30 rooms filled with parquet floors, stained-glass windows, ornate stenciling, and hand-carved woodwork. Above the top floor, a tower provides excellent views of the town. Walking-tour maps of Cortland's Historic District can be picked up here.

Cortland Country Music Park

Part RV camp, part country-music mecca, this 18-acre site (1804 Truxton Rd./Rte. 13, one mile north of the I-88 intersection, 607/753-0377, www.cortlandcountrymusicpark.com) bills itself as the "great Nashville of the Northeast." During the summer, four or five concerts by such top performers as Roy Acuff and Kenny Rogers are staged, along with two-steppin' dance classes, square dances, and jamborees. The park offers live music by regional bands on weekends year-round, and special events including horseshoe tournaments, the Old Timers Show, and the Festival of Bands.

Largely built by volunteer fans, the music park was started up in 1975. Centered on a low-slung Opry barn, it is equipped with one of the largest dance floors in the Northeast, an outdoor stage, and a Hall of Fame Museum (open only during events). In the museum, you'll find everything from a black-sequined dress formerly owned by Tammy Wynette to white boots once worn by Roy Acuff.

Shopping

It's worth traveling about eight miles south of Cortland to visit the **Book Barn of the Finger Lakes** (198 North Rd., Dryden, 607/844-9365, 10 A.M.–5:30 P.M. Mon.–Sat., noon–5 P.M.

Sun.). The sprawling 1850s barn houses nearly 98,000 used, rare, and scholarly books. It is run by Vladimer Dragan, who buys and sells all his books in person, even making house calls to estates and libraries. The bookstore is located off Route 13 opposite the Tompkins-Cortland Community College.

Accommodations

Greek Peak Mountain Resort and Hope Lake Lodge and Indoor Waterpark (2000 Rte. 392, 877/965-6343, www.greekpeak .net, $340 fireplace suite for 2–4 people) is a newly opened four season resort catering to skiers, families, and spa lovers. There are waterpark-inclusive packages and accommodations tailored to guests' individual interests. The resort offers three restaurants, over 30 ski trails, a tubing center, Nordic skiing and snowshoeing, while onsite full service Waterfalls Spa gives non-snowbunnies plenty of treatments to enjoy.

Owasco Lake Area

The smallest of the major Finger Lakes, Owasco is 12 miles long and 1.5 miles wide at its widest point. Iroquois for "the crossing," it lies 720 feet above sea level. For great views of Owasco, take Route 38 south, hugging the western shore, or Route 38A south, which travels high above the lake to the east. A few miles down, Route 38A bumps into Rockefeller Road, a shoreline route lined with 150-year-old camps and houses.

At the northern end of Owasco sits the city of Auburn, population 31,200. At the southern end are the village of Moravia, birthplace of President Millard Fillmore, the Fillmore Glen State Park, and miles of farm country.

AUBURN

For a small industrial city, Auburn has been home to an unusually high number of remarkable men and women. Among them are Logan, or Tahgahjute, the Iroquois orator; Harriet Tubman, the African American leader; William H. Seward, the visionary statesman; Thomas Mott Osborne, the pioneer of prison reform; and Theodore W. Case, the inventor of sound film. Tributes to all can be found in the city.

Before the invasion of the whites, Auburn was a Cayuga Indian village established at the junction of two trails. Revolutionary War veteran Col. John Hardenbergh arrived in 1793 and built the area's first gristmill. By 1810, the budding village boasted 90 dwellings, 17 mills, and an incorporated library containing 200 books.

The opening of the Auburn State Prison in 1817 and the Auburn Theological Seminary in 1821 greatly stimulated growth, and by the mid-1800s, Auburn was thriving. It even entertained hopes of becoming the state capital. The impressive public buildings on Capitol Street and lavish private homes on State Street date back to those heady days.

Seward House

One of the most interesting house museums in New York is this stately 1816 Federal-style home shaded by leafy trees (33 South St., 315/252-1283, www.sewardhouse.org, 10 A.M.–4 P.M. Tues.–Sat. and 1–4 P.M. Sun. July–Oct., 10 A.M–4 P.M. Tues.–Sat. Oct.–June, closed Jan., adults $7, seniors $6, students $2, under 10 free). The house belonged to William H. Seward, ardent abolitionist, New York governor, and U.S. senator, best remembered for purchasing Alaska from the Russians in 1857. Seward also served as Lincoln's secretary of state and was almost assassinated by a co-conspirator of John Wilkes Booth at the same time as the president.

Amazingly, almost everything in the Seward house is original. Inside you'll find not only Seward's furniture, but his grocery bills, top hats, pipe collection, snuff-box collection, 10,000 books, political campaign buttons, tea from the Boston Tea Party, personal letters from

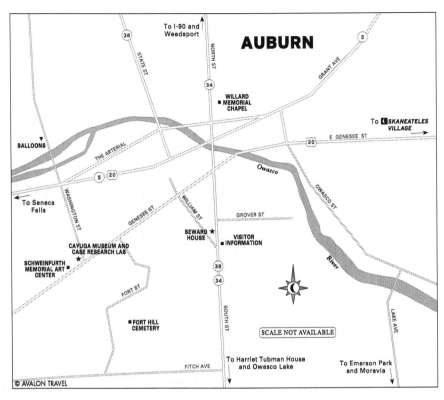

Abraham Lincoln, and calling cards of former visitors Horace Greeley, Frederick Douglass, Millard Fillmore, and Daniel Webster.

Seward first moved to Auburn for the love of Miss Frances Miller, whose father, Judge Elijah Miller, built the house. As a newly minted lawyer, Seward got a job in the judge's law firm, and proposed to his daughter. The ornery judge allowed the liaison on one condition: Seward could never take his daughter away from him. Seward agreed and, despite his enormous worldly success, lived under his father-in-law's thumb for the next 27 years.

Excellent guides bring the past alive and a fascinating collection of visiting leaders makes for a fun Guess Who game. Perhaps the most interesting aspect of the museum is the revelation and proof, in the form of photographs, news clippings, an eye witness account, and a bloodied, rent garment, that Lincoln was not a solo target that fateful night in the theater.

Harriet Tubman Home

On the outskirts of Auburn, next door to the AME Zion Church, stands a brick house and adjacent white clapboard house wrapped with a long front porch (180 South St., 315/252-2081, 10 A.M.–4 P.M. Tues.–Fri. and 10 A.M.–3 P.M. Sat. Feb.–Oct., last tour one hour before closing, adults $4.50, seniors $3, children $1.50). Harriet Tubman, known as the "Moses of her people," settled here after the Civil War, largely because her close friend and fellow abolitionist William Seward lived nearby.

Born a slave in Maryland in 1820 or 1821, Tubman escaped in 1849, fleeing first to Philadelphia and then to Canada. Yet as long as others remained in captivity, her freedom

© SASCHA ZUGER

Community-supported agriculture groups play a large part in Finger Lakes culinary culture.

meant little to her. During the next dozen years, she risked 19 trips south, rescuing more than 300 slaves. She mostly traveled alone and at night. Her motto was 'Keep going; children, if you are tired, keep going; if you are scared, keep going; if you are hungry, keep going; if you want to taste freedom, keep going.'

A visit to the Tubman property begins in a small museum exhibiting displays on famous African American women and a video on Tubman's life. Afterward, a member of the AME Zion Church takes visitors on a tour of the clapboard house where Tubman tended to the elderly and where a few of her belongings—including her bed and Bible—are on display. Tubman herself lived in the brick house, which is not open to the public.

Fort Hill Cemetery
Harriet Tubman, William Seward, and numerous other Auburn notables are buried in the Fort Hill Cemetery (19 Fort St., 315/253-8132, 9 A.M.–4 P.M. Mon.–Fri.), on a hill to the west side of State Street. Native Americans used the site as burial grounds as early as A.D. 1100.

A large stone fortress-gate marks the cemetery entrance, while inside towers the 56-foot-high **Logan Monument**. Erected upon a mound believed to be an ancient Native American altar, the monument pays homage to Logan, or Tahgahjute, the famed Cayuga orator born near Auburn in 1727. Logan befriended the European settlers until 1774, when a group of marauding Englishmen massacred his entire family in the Ohio Valley. In retaliation, he scalped more than 30 white men. Later that same year in Virginia, at a conference with the British, he gave one of the most moving speeches in early American history. "Logan never felt fear," he said. "He will not turn his heel to save his life. Who is there to mourn for Logan? Not one."

Cayuga Museum and Case Research Lab
Housed in a musty Greek Revival mansion, the Cayuga Museum (203 Genesee St., 315/253-8051, noon–5 P.M. Tues.– Sun. Feb.–Dec., suggested donation $3) is devoted to local history. Exhibits cover early Native American culture,

the Civil War, the Auburn Correctional Facility, Millard Fillmore, and women's rights.

Behind the museum mansion stands a simple, low-slung building known as the Case Research Lab (noon–4:30 P.M. Tues.– Sun. Feb.–Dec.). Here, in 1923, Theodore W. Case and E. I. Sponable invented the first commercially successful sound film, ushering in the movie era. Displays include the first sound camera and projector, original lab equipment, and Case's correspondence with Thomas Edison and Lee De Forest, a self-promoter who claimed *he* was the inventor of sound film.

Schweinfurth Memorial Art Center

Behind the Cayuga Museum, a modest art center (205 Genesee St., 315/255-1553, www.schweinfurthartcenter.org, 10 A.M.–5 P.M. Tues.–Sat., 1–5 P.M. Sun., closed Jan., admission by donation) features temporary exhibits by contemporary and classic artists. Shows feature everything from fine art and photography to folk art and architecture. Each winter the museum hosts a popular quilt show.

Willard Memorial Chapel

The only complete Tiffany chapel known to exist, the Willard Memorial (17 Nelson St., 315/252-0339, 10 A.M.–4 P.M. Tues.–Fri. and summer Sat. mornings, suggested donation $3) glows with the muted, bejeweled light of 15 windows handcrafted by the Tiffany Glass and Decorating Company. Louis C. Tiffany also designed the chapel's handsome oak furniture inlaid with mosaics, leaded-glass chandeliers, and gold-stenciled pulpit.

A visit to the chapel begins with a video on the chapel's history and the now-defunct Auburn Theological Seminary of which it was once a part. In July and August, free organ recitals and concerts are played in the chapel.

Accommodations and Food

One mile south of Auburn you'll find the **Springside Inn** (41 W. Lake Rd./Rte. 38, 315/252-7247, www.springsideinn.com $100–150, with continental breakfast), a striking red Victorian with big white porches. Upstairs are a half-dozen renovated guest rooms furnished with antiques and nice touches like canopy beds, clawfoot or whirlpool tubs, and a complimentary Finger Lakes wine basket on arrival.

The inn is best known for its restaurant (open for dinner and Sunday brunch only, $9–20), which is a local favorite for special occasions. On the menu are such traditional American dishes as shrimp Newburg, Long Island Duck, steak, and lobster.

Balloons (65 Washington St., across from the state prison, 315/252-9761) is a friendly spot with an art deco decor, serving heaping platters of Italian food since 1934.

The Restaurant at Elderberry Pond (3728 Center Street Rd. 315/252-6025, www.elderberrypond.com, $24) is surrounded by 100-acres of organic ingredients, from herbs to free range meats, grown right on Elderberry Pond Farm. The menu changes daily but a sampling includes items like garden fresh ratatouille and pasture-raised pork with apple cider puree. The fresh ingredients are not cheap; sandwiches and salads start at $11. The adjacent farm store located in an 1800s smokehouse is a good spot to pick up some favorites for the road.

MORAVIA

Well off the beaten track, this small village boasts a number of handsome 19th-century buildings and the 1820s **St. Matthew's Episcopal Church** (14 Church St., 315/497-3747, 8 A.M.–5 P.M., tours by appointment). The sanctuary's interior is covered with elaborate oak carvings designed and executed in Oberammergau, Germany.

Fillmore Glen State Park

Just south of the village of Moravia lies the 857-acre Fillmore Glen State Park (Rte. 38, 315/497-0130, dawn–dusk daily, $6–8 parking), centered on a deep and rugged ravine with five spectacular waterfalls. At the foot of the main falls is a geometric rock formation known as the Cowpens, and a popular swimming hole. Nearby await hiking trails, a campground, and a playground. For campground reservations, call 800/456-CAMP.

The park also contains a replica of the tiny log cabin in which President Millard Fillmore was born. His actual birthplace lies about five miles east of the park. Fillmore grew up dirt poor and went to work at an early age; he later described his upbringing as "completely shut out from the enterprises of civilization and advancement."

Cayuga Lake Area

The longest of the Finger Lakes, Cayuga stretches out for 38 moody miles, 381 feet above sea level. It varies in depth from a few feet to 435 feet, and supports a wide variety of marine life. In shallow waters swim carp and large-mouth bass; in deeper ones, northern pike and lake trout.

Iroquois for "boat landing," Cayuga was named after the Iroquois nation that originally lived along and farmed its shores. The Cayugas were called Gue-u-gweh-o-no, or people of the muckland, exemplified by the once-enormous Montezuma Marsh at the northern end of the lake.

Today, just south of the marsh, sits Seneca Falls, the small industrial town where the first Women's Rights Convention met in 1848. Anchoring the southern end of the lake is Ithaca, a friendly cultural center that's home to Cornell University, Ithaca College, and craggy gorges with waterfalls higher than Niagara. Along the lake's western shores are a half-dozen wineries; on the eastern shores, the historic village of Aurora.

SENECA FALLS

Seneca Falls owes its early development to a series of waterfalls dropping over 50 feet. The first gristmill was built here in 1795, and by the 1840s, the town supported dozens of water-powered factories. Many employed women worked 14-hour days for wages they had to turn over to their husbands. In 1840s America, women were not allowed to own money or property or to even serve as legal guardians of their own children.

Elizabeth Cady Stanton and her abolitionist husband Henry Stanton moved to Seneca Falls from Boston in 1847, a time when Seneca Falls was a major transportation hub and the Finger Lakes were a center for the abolitionist movement. Often home alone, caring for her children, Stanton felt isolated and overwhelmed by housework. She also noticed the worse plight of her poorer neighbors: "Alas! alas!," she wrote in her autobiography *Eighty Years and More,* "Who can measure the mountains of sorrow and suffering endured in unwelcome motherhood in the abodes of ignorance, poverty, and vice. . . ."

On July 13, 1848, Stanton shared her discontent with four friends; then and there the

a Finger Lakes field, seen from a hot air balloon

© SASCHA ZUGER

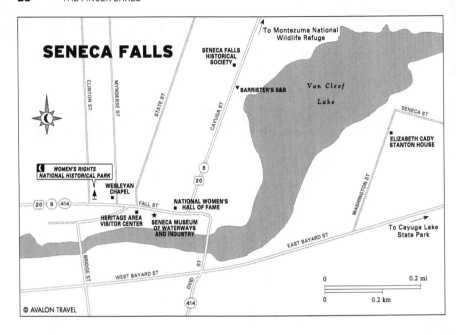

group decided to convene a discussion on the status of women. They set a date for six days thence and published announcements in the local papers. About 300 people— men and women—showed up, a Declaration of Sentiments was issued, and the women deemed the convention a success. They were little prepared for the nationwide storm of outrage and ridicule that followed. Their lives, the town of Seneca Falls, and the nation would never be the same.

Seneca Falls centers around Fall Street (Rtes. 5 and 20). Running parallel is the Seneca River and the Cayuga-Seneca Canal, which links Cayuga and Seneca Lakes. At the eastern end of town is the artificially constructed Van Cleef Lake.

Heritage Area Visitors Center

For a good general introduction to Seneca Falls, stop into this center (115 Fall St., 315/568-6894, 10 A.M.–4 P.M. Mon.–Sat., noon–4 P.M. Sun., free admission). The exhibits cover virtually every aspect of the town's history, from its

Iroquois beginnings and early factory days to its women's history and ethnic heritage.

Seneca Falls is one of New York State's Heritage Areas—loosely designated historic districts linked by a common theme. The Seneca Falls theme is reform movements, but the center pays at least equal attention to the town's industrial past. Seneca Falls once held world fame for its knitting mills and pump factories, several of which still operate.

Don't leave the center without learning about the destruction of the city's once invaluable waterfalls. The falls were eliminated in 1915 to create the Cayuga-Seneca Canal and, by extension, Van Cleef Lake. The flooding destroyed more than 150 buildings, and today, many foundations are still visible beneath the lake's clear waters.

Women's Rights National Historical Park

Down the street from the visitors center stand the ruins of the **Wesleyan Chapel** (126 Fall St.), where the historic 1848 convention took place. Alas, all that remains of the church today are two fragile brick walls and a piece of roof, though a new project to preserve the site by completing the building (while allowing visitors to see the original portions) is expected to be completed by the end of 2010. The nearby 140-foot-long wall and fountain bears the Declaration of Sentiments: "We hold these truths to be self-evident; that all men and women are created equal. . . ."

Across the street from the chapel, in the spacious, two-story **Women's Rights Visitor Center** (136 Fall St., 315/568-2991, 9 A.M.–5 P.M. daily, adults $3, under 17 free), you'll find exhibits on the convention, its leaders, and the times in which they lived. Other sections focus on such women's issues as employment, marriage, fashion, and sports. There's a lot of interesting information here, along with free handouts and a good bookstore.

Elizabeth Cady Stanton House

Also part of the Women's Rights National Historic Park, the Stanton house (32 Washington St., tours daily June–Sept., $1 pp) is about a mile from the visitors center on the other side of Van Cleef Lake. Stanton lived here with her husband and seven children from 1846 to 1862. During much of that time, she wrote extensively about women's rights.

Among the many reformers who frequented the Stanton home was Amelia Bloomer, the woman who popularized the pantaloons that bear her name. Though a resident of Seneca Falls, Bloomer did not sign the Declaration of Sentiments, believing it to be too radical.

Today, the airy Stanton home has been meticulously restored. Few furnishings remain, but everything is authentic, including the bronze cast of Stanton's hand clasping that of Susan B. Anthony's. Stanton met Anthony soon after the 1848 convention, and the women worked closely together throughout their lives.

In the summer months, house tours are offered daily; visitors must sign up for the tours at the Women's Rights Visitor Center (136 Fall St., 315/568-2991).

Mary Baker Eddy Museum

One block down from the Women's Rights National Historical Park stands a small museum dedicated to the life of Mary Baker Eddy (118 Fall St., 315/568-6488, www.marybakereddy.com, 10 A.M.–4 P.M. Tues.–Sun., library: free admission; exhibits: adults $6 adults, seniors and children 6–17 $4, children under 6 free). Interactive displays document the life of this 19th-century woman who challenged conventional thinking in theology, science, and medicine.

Seneca Museum of Waterways and Industry

Housed in a historic building, this museum (89 Fall St., 315/568-1510, www.senecamuseum.com, 10 A.M.–4 P.M. Tues.–Sat. year-round, and noon–4 P.M. Sun. mid-June–Aug., adults $2, families $5) is filled with exhibits on the history of the village and its surrounding waterways. A colorful 35-foot mural lines one wall, while elsewhere are antique fire engines, pumps, looms, and printing presses. One exhibit shows how the Erie Canal was built, another is a working lock model.

National Women's Hall of Fame

The Women's Hall of Fame (76 Fall St., 315/568-8060, www.greatwomen.org, 10 A.M.–5 P.M. Mon.–Sat. and noon–5 P.M. Sun. May–Sept., 11 A.M.–5 P.M. Wed.–Sat. Oct.–Apr., adults $3, seniors and students $1.50, children under 6 free) bills itself as "the only national membership organization devoted exclusively to the accomplishments of American women." Blown-up photos and plaques pay homage to everyone from painter Mary Cassatt to anthropologist Margaret Mead.

Seneca Falls Historical Society

Formerly known as the Mynderse/Partridge/Becker House, this museum (55 Cayuga St., 315/568-8412, 9 A.M.–4 P.M. Mon.–Fri. year-round, noon–4 P.M. Sat.–Sun. in summer, adults $3, seniors and students $1.50, families $7) is housed in a notable Queen Anne home, set back from the street behind an iron fence. Inside, 23 elegant rooms feature period furnishings, elaborate woodwork, and an extensive costume collection. A rare collection of 19th-century circus toys is strewn through the children's playroom.

Montezuma National Wildlife Refuge

Five miles east of Seneca Falls is the Montezuma Wildlife Refuge (3395 Rtes. 5 and 20E [Exit 40 or 41 off I-90], 315/568-5987, dawn–dusk daily Apr.–Nov., free admission), a haven for migrating and nesting birds. Spread out over 6,300 acres of swamplands, marshlands, and fields, the refuge includes a visitors center, nature trail, driving trail, and two observation towers. Nearly 315 species of birds have been spotted in the refuge since it was established in 1937. Migrating waterfowl arrive by the tens of thousands in mid-April and early October. Late May to early June is a good time to spot warblers; in mid-September, the refuge fills with shorebirds and wading birds.

Before the turn of the century, Montezuma Marsh was many times its current size, stretching about 12 miles long and up to 8 miles wide. The Erie Canal and Cayuga Lake dam projects greatly reduced its size.

Cayuga Lake State Park

Three miles east of Seneca Falls lies the 190-acre Cayuga Lake State Park (off Rte. 89, 315/568-5163, dawn–dusk daily, parking $6–8), offering a swimming beach, a bathhouse, hiking trails, a playground, and a 287-site campground. In the late 1700s, the park was part of a Cayuga Indian reservation, and in the late 1800s it was a resort area serviced by a train from Seneca Falls. The state park was established here in 1928. To reserve a campsite, call 800/456-CAMP.

Finger Lakes National Forest

The 16,212 acre Finger Lakes National Forest (National Forest Headquarters, 5218 rte 414 Hector, 607/546-4470) lies between Seneca and Cayuga Lakes is the state's sole National Forest. Gorges, woods, pastures, shrub lands and many wildlife ponds are intermingled to provide excellent opportunities for wildlife viewing and fishing, with permit. Over 30 miles of trails, including the 12 mile Interloken Trail, which is part of the **Finger Lakes Trail,** allow for hiking and horseback riding in the warm months and snowmobiling and Nordic skiing in the winter. Apples, raspberries and other fruits are abundant throughout the forest, with five acres managed specifically for blueberry bushes. Free camping can be had on three developed campgrounds on a first-come, first-served basis.

Events

The **Convention Days Celebration** (800/732-1848, www.conventiondays.com), commemorating the first Women's Rights Convention, takes place on the weekend closest to July 19–20. Featured are concerts, dances, speeches, historical tours, food, kids' events, and a re-enactment of the signing of the Declaration of Sentiments.

Accommodations and Food

Several lovely B&Bs are in the heart of Seneca Falls. The 1855 **Hubbell House** (42 Cayuga St., 315/568-9690, www.hubbellhousebb.com, $115–145), built in "Gothic cottage" style, overlooks Van Cleef Lake. Downstairs are a large double parlor, library, and dining room; upstairs are four guest rooms furnished with antiques.

The 1825 **Van Cleef Homestead B&B** (86 Cayuga St., 315/568-2275, www.flare.net/vancleef, $95–120) was built by Seneca Falls' first permanent resident, Lawrence Van Cleef. It's a Federal-style home offering three comfortable, air-conditioned guest rooms and a swimming pool.

The large, historic ❰ **Barristers Bed and Breakfast** (56 Cayuga St., 800/914-6145, www.sleepbarristers.com, $120–170), built by master craftsmen in the 1800s, features five spacious guest rooms furnished with antiques, a large front porch, cozy common room, and stone patio with a fire pit, perfect for sitting around on cool evenings. Guest amenities include a refreshment center.

The fresh, modern **Hotel Clarence** (108 Falls St., 315/712-4000, www.hotelclarence.com, $109–189), recently opened by an executive chef and management team formerly with the Mirbeau Inn and Spa (in Skaneateles), plays on the town's historic place as inspiration for 'It's a Wonderful Life' both in name and in the large live art-installation-like showing of the black and white movie on one wall of the entrance. A variety of 48 rooms and suites with clean contemporary lines and extensive amenities (robes, Keurig coffee machines, Ipod docking stations, cordless multi-line phones, etc.) are upstairs while excellent dining at **DIVINE Kitchen and Bar** (average entrée $19) and a hipsterish bar experience await downstairs, where every time you ring a bellman, a barfly gets their wings' (Smoked, with Maytag Blue, Apple and Jicama, of course.) Award-winning Chef Ed Moro uses the freshest of regional goods in his innovative take on foodie favorites in a funky casual/elegant setting.

WATERLOO

A few miles west of Seneca Falls on Routes 5 and 20 is Waterloo, a surprisingly busy village filled with aging red-brick buildings and shady trees. As a plaque along Main Street attests, Waterloo claims to be the birthplace of Memorial Day. Originally known as Declaration Day, the event apparently first took place here on May 5, 1866, in honor of the Civil War dead. Flags flew at half-mast, businesses closed, and a solemn parade marched down Main Street. In 1966, the U.S. Congress and President Johnson officially recognized Waterloo as the birthplace of Memorial Day.

In the middle of town reigns the **Terwilliger Museum** (31 E. Main St., 315/539-0533, 1–4 P.M. Tues.–Fri.). Here you'll find a reconstructed Native American longhouse and village store, along with antique pianos, carriages, fire equipment, and a 1914 Waterloo mural.

AURORA

Halfway down Cayuga's expansive eastern shore is picture-perfect Aurora, its houses laid out like beads on a string. Most date back to the mid-1800s; the entire village is on the National Register of Historic Places.

Called Deawendote, or Village of Constant Dawn, by the Cayuga, Aurora attracted its first white settlers in the late 1780s. Henry Wells founded Wells College here in 1868, and the school—a premier liberal arts college for women that only went coed in 2005—remains a focal point of Main Street.

Also in Aurora is **MacKenzie-Childs** (3260 N. Main St./Rte. 90, 315/364-7123, 9:30 A.M.–6 P.M. daily, call for studio tour information), a classy home-furnishings-design studio best known for its whimsical terracotta pottery. The studio employs about 100 craftspeople, who design everything from glassware to lamps, and is housed on a 19th-century estate with great views of the lake.

In the Tudor style Aurora Free Library building, the charming, turn-of-the-century **Morgan Opera House** (Rte. 90 at Cherry Ave., 315/364-5437, May–Sept.) offers musical and dramatic events.

Accommodations and Food

In the center of Aurora presides the lovely 1833 **Aurora Inn** (391 Main St./Rte. 90, www.aurorainn.com, $200–350). Owned by Wells College, the red-brick inn with its wide white balconies and well-groomed gardens was recently restored. Inside, find 10 luxurious guest rooms furnished with antiques and oriental rugs, a waterside restaurant (average entrée $22) with views of the lake, and a cozy tavern with a fireplace and mahogany bar. On the menu of the highly-thought-of restaurant is classic American cuisine.

E.B. Morgan House (431 Main St., 315/364-8888, $225–325), also operated by the Aurora Inn, rents rooms individually or all seven for larger groups. When the entire house is rented, a private epicurean dinner option ($100 pp) for up to 14 is available via the Aurora Inn's Executive Chef Greg Rhoad.

For more casual dining, **Pumpkin Hill Bistro** (2051 Rte. 90, 315/364-7091, $9–14), housed in an 1820s hand-built dwelling, was transported to its current location in 2001. Burgers, paninis, and country favorites are enhanced by regional farm goods. Nightly specials and harvest brunches bring in a steady flow of locals.

ROMULUS

Midway down the west side of the lake lies Romulus, known for its vineyards and wineries. Two of the best, only five miles apart, are the **Swedish Hill Vineyard** (4565 Rte. 414, 315/549-8326, www.swedishhill.com) and the **Knapp Winery, Vineyards, and Restaurant** (2770 County Rd. 128, 607/869-9271, www.knappwine.com). Swedish Hill, a very large operation, produces about 30,000 cases of 25 different kinds of wines a year; Knapp is much smaller, but its wines are among the region's finest. Both wineries are open April–December, Monday–Saturday 10 A.M.–5 P.M. and Sunday noon–5 P.M.; call for off-season hours.

The breezy **Knapp Winery Restaurant** (2770 County Rd. 128, 607/869-9481, average lunch entrée $9, average dinner entrée $18) serves lunch daily April–October and dinner on summer weekends; call for hours. Local produce is emphasized.

OVID

Heading south of Romulus on Route 96, you'll come to the hamlet of Ovid, astride a small ridge surrounded by farmland. In the heart of the village stand three red-brick Greek Revival buildings known as the **Three Bears** because of how they diminish progressively in size. The "Papa Bear" was once the county courthouse; "Mama Bear," the village library; and "Baby Bear," the county jail. Today, the buildings house county offices.

Accommodations and Camping

Off Route 89 overlooking Cayuga Lake is **Sned-Acres Campground** (6590 Cayuga Lake Rd., 607/869-9787), a good place for families, as it's equipped with a playground and miniature golf course.

Nearby lies the **Driftwood Inn** (Rte. 89, Sheldrake-on-Cayuga, 607/532-4324, $105–145 d), offering four guest rooms in the main house, two efficiency units, and two housekeeping cottages. Out front is a 260-foot-long

waterfront equipped with small boats and views of the lake.

The **Tillinghast Manor B&B** (7246 S. Main St., 607/869-3584, $85–100) is a palatial Victorian mansion with a square central tower, an inviting porch, and a large circular drive. Inside you'll find a grand walnut staircase and five spacious guest rooms with king-size beds.

TRUMANSBURG

About 10 miles north of Ithaca thunder **Taughannock Falls,** a skinny but dazzling 215-foot-long stream of water flanked on either side by towering stone walls. Just 10,000 years ago, the falls cascaded straight down into Cayuga Lake, but erosion has moved them almost a mile inland. Thirty feet higher than Niagara, Taughannock Falls are the highest straight falls east of the Rockies.

The falls are situated within the 783-acre **Taughannock Falls State Park** (Rte. 89, 607/387-6739, dawn–dusk daily, parking $6–8), which also offers lake swimming, fishing, boating, hiking, cabins, and a 76-site campground. Children will enjoy the park's imaginative playground, equipped with wooden towers and platforms. For campground reservations, call 800/456-CAMP. An overlook before the park gate offers a nice chance to see the falls without a commitment for those short on time.

Entertainment and Events

One of the top music clubs in the region is the **Rongovian Embassy to the U.S.A.** (Rte. 96, 607/387-3334, www.rong.com), a big, comfortable, laid-back joint with live jazz, rock, reggae, country, or blues most nights of the week. Tasty Mexican food is served.

In July and August, free jazz, Latin, folk, and rock concerts take place weekly in **Taughannock Falls State Park** (Rte. 89, 607/387-6739).

Accommodations

Two lovely options close to Taughannock Falls are the best bet for this area. The proximity to Ithaca (10 minutes) makes this peaceful alternate locale worthy of consideration for a base to explore the city.

©SASCHA ZUGER

Taughannock Falls

The Halsey House (2547 Trumansburg Rd., 607/387-5428, www.halseyhouse.com, $199–229) sits at the entrance to the Falls road and offers that perfect mix of romantic elegance and modern convenience (Wi-Fi, flatscreen TVs with a broad DVD collection, robes, individual air-conditioning, complimentary snacks and drinks) in sumptuous bedded rooms with gorgeous upscale whirlpool bathrooms. Lovely innkeepers, cozy fireplace common areas, and the included gourmet breakfast add to the experience.

Inn at Gothic Eves (112 E. Main, 607/387-6033, www.gothiceves.com, $149–199) is an 1855 inn nestled in the heart of the tiny village. This unique property offers a selection of rooms (from Victorian to the recently renovated Potter House fireplace suites) and a true farm-to-table breakfast using eggs, berries, and local cheeses, often harvested that very morning. A can't miss at this spot is a session in the outdoor wood-fired hot tub, included in the stay and stoked by the innkeeper by appointment.

Ithaca

At the southern tip of Cayuga Lake lies Ithaca, a small, progressive university town whose population of about 30,000 nearly doubles in size whenever its two colleges—Cornell University and Ithaca College—are in session. This is the kind of laid-back place where everyone wears Birkenstocks and reads Proust in outdoor cafés.

Ithaca was originally a Cayuga settlement that was destroyed during General Sullivan's ruthless 1779 campaign. The first white settlers arrived in 1788, but the town didn't really begin to grow until the opening of Cornell University in 1868.

For several years beginning in 1914, Ithaca was a center for the motion picture business. The Wharton Studios based itself here; *Exploits of Elaine*, starring Lionel Barrymore and Pearl White, and *Patria*, starring Irene Castle, were both filmed in Ithaca. The region's unpredictable weather proved less than ideal for moviemaking, however, and in 1920 the industry moved west.

Ithaca also claims to be the birthplace of the sundae, supposedly first concocted here in 1891. "As the story goes," writes Arch Merrill in *Slim Fingers Beckon,* "an Ithaca preacher came into C. C. Platt's drugstore, weary and sweating after the Sunday morning service. He asked the druggist to fix a dish of ice cream and pour some syrup on it…and thus another American institution was born."

Orientation

Idyllically situated at the edge of Cayuga Lake, Ithaca is all but surrounded by steep hills and gorges. Three powerful waterfalls plunge right through the heart of the city.

The downtown is small, low-slung, and compact. In its flat center lies **Ithaca Commons,** a pedestrian mall spread out along State Street. Perched on a steep hill to the east is Cornell University. The roller-coaster streets surrounding Cornell are known as **Collegetown.** On another hill to the south sits Ithaca College.

The best way to explore Ithaca and environs is by foot and car. Street parking is generally available, but there are also three downtown municipal garages.

SIGHTS
Ithaca Commons

The pedestrian-only Commons runs along State Street between Aurora and Cayuga Streets and along Tioga Street between Seneca and State Streets. Somewhat European in feel, it's filled with fountains, trees, flowers, and benches, and is flanked with shops and restaurants. At the western end is **Clinton House** (116 N. Cayuga St.), a historic hotel now housing various arts organizations and the Ticket Center.

Most of the buildings along the Commons were built between the 1860s and the 1930s. Note the handsome Italianate building at **No. 158 East State Street,** and the art deco storefront at **No. 152 East State Street.** Just beyond the Commons, at **No. 101 West State Street,** glows a 1947 neon sign of a cocky chanticleer.

The **Sagan Planet Walk** was built in memory of astronomer Carl Sagan. It starts at the "sun" on the Commons and continues on to visit nine "planets" along a three-quarter-mile route leading to the ScienCenter Museum. Visitors who get their "Passport to the Solar System" stamped along the way earn a free visit to the museum.

DeWitt Mall

One block north of the Commons, at the corner of Seneca and Cayuga Streets, is the DeWitt Mall. This former school building now contains about 20 shops, galleries, and restaurants, including the famed **Moosewood Restaurant** (607/273-9610). Among the galleries are the **Sola Art Gallery** (607/272-6552, 10:30 A.M.–5:30 P.M. Mon.–Sat.), which specializes in graphic arts, and the **Upstairs Gallery** (607/272-8614, 11 A.M.–3 P.M. Tues.–Sat.), exhibiting the work of area artists, many affiliated with Cornell or Ithaca College.

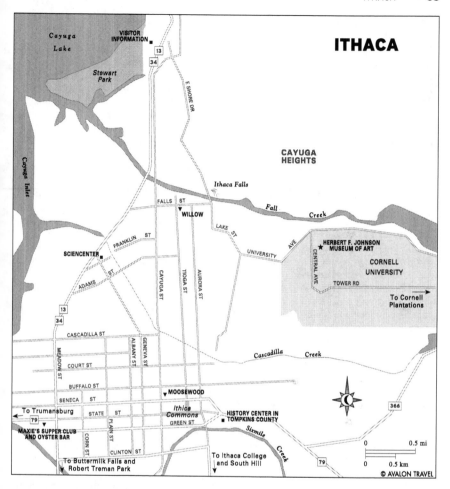

Historic DeWitt Park

The oldest buildings in the city are located on or near DeWitt Park, a peaceful retreat at East Buffalo and North Cayuga Streets one block north of DeWitt Mall. Many buildings in this National Historic District date back to the early 1800s.

On the park's north side stands the 1817 **Old Courthouse** (121 E. Court St., 607/273-8284), thought to be the oldest Gothic Revival building in the state; and the **First Presbyterian Church,** designed by James Renwick, the architect of St. Patrick's Cathedral in New York City. On the east side is the Romanesque **First Baptist Church,** built in 1890.

Other Downtown Galleries

The eight-room **Asia House Gallery and Museum** (118 S. Meadow St., 607/272-8850) specializes in the traditional fine arts, decorative arts, and antique folk arts of Asia. **Handwork** (102 W. State St., 607/273-9400) showcases the work of 25 local craftspeople.

History Center in Tompkins County

Inside this large, renovated building you'll find a fine historical museum (401 E. State St., at Seneca and Green Sts., 607/273-8284, 11 A.M.–5 P.M. Tues., Thurs., and Sat., free admission) run by the DeWitt Historical Society. The society owns an impressive collection of over 20,000 objects, 3,000 books, and 100,000 photographs.

Permanent displays show the city's beginnings, its industries, and its surprising film history. Temporary exhibits focus on such subjects as folk arts, alternative medicine, Italian immigrants, and Finnish-American saunas.

The ScienCenter

The hands-on ScienCenter (601 1st St., at Franklin St., 607/272-0600, www.sciencenter.org, 10 A.M.–5 P.M. Tues.–Sat., noon–5 P.M. Sun., adults $6, children 3–17 $4) primarily appeals to young ones, but adults can learn something here as well. Walk into a camera for a zoom-lens view of how it works. Draw your own picture on a "harmonograph." Measure the electrical current running through your body. Or, play outdoor mini-golf on the Galaxy Golf Course. Pre-schoolers will want to explore the Curiosity Corner, while older kids will probably head to the animal room or space exhibits.

The ScienCenter was largely created by volunteers, many of them Cornell scientists and engineers, which helps account for its homey yet high-tech feel. Out back is an imaginative wooden playground filled with games that teach kids about physical principles such as gravity and heat.

Ithaca Falls

At the corner of Falls and Lake Streets thunder Ithaca Falls, the last and greatest of the six waterfalls along the mile-long Fall Creek gorge. These "pulpit falls" are closely-spaced rapids created by layers of resistant rock. To reach the site from Ithaca Commons—about a 20-minute walk—head north along Cayuga Street to Falls Street and turn right. To one side is a small grassy park and a wooded path that leads to a popular fishing hole.

Cornell University

High on a hill overlooking downtown Ithaca presides Cornell University, built around a long, lush green lined with ivy-covered buildings. The views from here are especially fine at twilight, when Cayuga's waters glow with the setting sun and the gorges begin a slow fade into black.

Cornell was founded in 1865 by Ezra Cornell and Andrew D. White, who vowed to establish an "institution where any person can find instruction in any study." In so doing, they challenged a number of long-standing mores. Their university was one of the first to be nonsectarian; to offer instruction to all qualified applicants, regardless of sex, race, or class; and to feature courses in everything from agriculture to the classics.

Traffic and information booths are located at each entrance to the central campus. Except in a few metered areas, parking is by permit only; purchase a permit at the traffic booths. Visitors to the Herbert F. Johnson Museum can park in metered spaces out front. To tour the campus, contact the **Information and Referral Center** (Day Hall, Tower Rd. and East Ave., 607/254-4636, www.cornell.edu).

HERBERT F. JOHNSON MUSEUM OF ART

At the northern end of the Cornell campus reigns the Johnson Museum of Art (University Ave., 607/255-6464, www.museum.cornell.edu, 10 A.M.–5 P.M. Tues.–Sun., free admission), housed in a striking modern building designed by I. M. Pei. The museum features especially strong collections of Asian and contemporary art but is also a teaching museum, containing a little bit of almost everything.

The Asian collection is situated on the 5th floor, where big picture windows open out onto 360-degree views of Cayuga Lake and the surrounding countryside. Among the many exquisite objects on display are funerary urns from the T'ang dynasty, silk paintings from 19th-century Japan, and bronze Buddhas from 15th-century Thailand.

AMONG THE MENNONITES

A surprisingly large number of Mennonite and Amish Mennonite communities are scattered throughout the Finger Lakes and Western New York. Some were established generations ago, but many others were set up over the past decade or two by people originally from Pennsylvania and Ohio, attracted to New York by its many recently abandoned family farms.

The Mennonite religion is a Protestant sect, founded by Dutch reformer Menno Simons in Switzerland in the 1500s. The Amish are the Mennonites' most conservative branch, established in Pennsylvania in the 18th century. Both groups shun modern society and technology.

Throughout the region, you'll see traffic signs alerting you to horse and buggies, and you'll spot occasional plaques advertising handmade quilts, furniture, or baskets for sale.

An especially large Amish population lives in Cattaraugus County in Western New York, while many Mennonites live in Yates, Schuyler, and Ontario Counties in the Finger Lakes. Local residents estimate that the Mennonite population in these last three counties – centered around Keuka Lake – has more than tripled in the past 15 years, to over 1,000.

Why the Amish and Mennonites have success as farmers when others have failed is a topic for debate. Many believe that it has to do with the "plain people's" smaller-size farms and low labor costs. In Mennonite communities, everyone in the family, from young children to great-grandparents, contributes to the operation of the farm.

The Amish and Mennonites dislike having their pictures taken. Please respect their wishes.

WILDER BRAIN COLLECTION

Those interested in the odd and macabre will want to step into Cornell's Uris Hall, East Avenue and Tower Road, and ride an elevator up to the second floor. In a small case to the rear of the building are the eight surviving stars of the Burt Green Wilder brain collection, which once numbered about 1,600 floating specimens.

Wilder was Cornell's first zoologist. He began assembling his collection in the late 1800s in the hopes of proving the size and shape of a person's brain were related to his or her race, sex, intelligence, and personality. Alas, his studies only disproved his theories, and in 1911 he rocked the scientific world by declaring that there was no difference between the brains of black and white men.

The pickled collection includes the extraordinarily large brain of criminal Edward Howard Ruloff, who was hanged in Binghamton on May 18, 1871. Ruloff allegedly killed his wife and daughter and was convicted of killing three men. He was also highly intelligent, and had published several scholarly papers despite his lack of formal education.

Burt Green Wilder's brain is also in the collection. Considerably smaller than Ruloff's, it sits yellowing in viscous formaldehyde. The creator has joined his creation.

CORNELL PLANTATIONS

Just north of the Cornell campus, a 2,800-acre oasis of green (1 Plantations Rd., off Rte. 366, 607/255-3020, dawn–dusk daily, free admission) encompasses an arboretum, specialty gardens devoted to everything from wildflowers to poisonous plants, and nature trails winding through the Fall Creek gorge. Pick up maps in the gift shop.

SAPSUCKER WOODS BIRD SANCTUARY

At the eastern edge of the city lies a world-class center for the study, appreciation, and conservation of birds. Not everything is open to the public, but key attractions include 4.2 miles of trails through the Sapsucker Woods Sanctuary and the Stuart Observatory, which overlooks a waterfowl pond and bird-feeding garden.

The 220-acre Sapsucker Woods were named by bird artist Louis Agassiz Fuertes in 1901 after he spotted a pair of yellow-bellied sapsuckers—unusual for the region—nesting in the area. Sapsuckers continue to breed here each year. Near the woods you'll find a **visitors center** (159 Sapsucker Woods Rd., 607/254-2473, www.birds.cornell.edu, 8 A.M.–5 P.M. Mon.–Thurs., 8 A.M.–4 P.M. Fri., 10 A.M.–4 P.M. Sat.) where you can pick up maps and view paintings by Agassiz Fuertes.

Buttermilk Falls State Park

Just south of downtown is Buttermilk Falls (Rte. 13, 607/273-5761, dawn–dusk daily May–Nov., parking $6–8), plummeting more than 500 feet past 10 waterfalls, churning rapids, sculptured pools, and raggedy cliffs. Alongside the falls runs a trail leading up to spirelike Pinnacle Rock and Treman Lake. At the base of the falls are a natural swimming hole, ball fields, and a campground. For campground reservations, call 800/456-CAMP.

Robert H. Treman State Park

Five miles south of Ithaca lies Treman Park (off Rte. 13, 607/273-3440, dawn–dusk daily Apr.–Nov., parking $6–8)—1,025 acres of wild and rugged beauty. Near the entrance is Enfield Glen, a forested gorge traversed by a stone pathway and steps. The steps lead to 115-foot-high Lucifer Falls and a vista stretching 1.5 miles down into a deep glen threaded by the Gorge Trail. A three-story 1839 gristmill, a natural swimming pool, and a campground are also on the grounds. For campground reservations, call 800/456-CAMP.

ENTERTAINMENT
Performing Arts

Cornell's **Schwartz Center for Theatre Arts** (430 College Ave., 607/254-2787) stages 6–12 plays September–May, along with the Cornell Dance Series and numerous guest performances. Professional regional theater is staged by the acclaimed **Hangar Theatre** (Rte. 89, Cass Park, 607/273-8588) June–August. The **Kitchen Theater** (607/272-0403) presents contemporary theater in the historic Clinton House (116 N. Cayuga St.).

Among the groups performing regularly in the city is the **Cayuga Chamber Orchestra** (116 N. Cayuga St., 607/273-8981), the official orchestra of Ithaca. The **Ithaca Ballet** (607/277-1967) performs both classical and contemporary works.

Nightlife

Good club listings can be found in the *Ithaca Times* (607/277-7000), a free alternative news weekly. One of the best music clubs in the area is the **Rongovian Embassy to the U.S.A.** (Rte. 96, 607/387-3334, www.rong.com) in nearby Trumansburg. The **ABC Cafe** (308 Stewart Ave., 607/277-4770) features folk music, a weekly open mike, and jazz on Sunday.

SPORTS AND RECREATION

Circle Greenway is a 10-mile walk that leads to many of Ithaca's foremost natural and urban attractions, including gorges, the waterfront, Cornell, and the Commons. A free map can be picked up at the Ithaca/Tompkins County Convention and Visitors Bureau (904 E. Shore Dr., near Stewart Park, 607/272-1313 or 800/284-8422, www.visitithaca.com).

Cayuga Lake Cruises (702 W. Buffalo St., 607/256-0898) offers dinner, lunch, brunch, and cocktail cruises aboard the M/V *Manhattan*. **Tiohero Tours** (607/697-0166 or 866/846-4376, www.tioherotours.com, 12 adults, $11 seniors, $8 children 5–12) offers narrated one-hour tours of the lake that depart from the Farmers Market pier at 11 A.M. and 12:30 P.M. Saturday and Sunday, from May to October.

ACCOMMODATIONS

As the teaching hotel of Cornell's School of Hotel Administration, the **Statler Hotel** (11 East Ave., Cornell University Campus, 607/257-2500 or 800/541-2501, www.statler-hotel.cornell.edu, $115–165 d) is Ithaca's hotel of choice for visiting parents, academics, and travelers. The hotel features 150 guest rooms and two restaurants; guests have access to most of Cornell's facilities, including the gym, pool, tennis courts, and golf course.

The very unique **Log Country Inn B&B** (4 LaRue Rd., at S. Danby Rd., 607/589-4771, www.logtv.com/inn, $70–150 d) may sound rustic but it features soaring cathedral ceilings, fireplaces, a sauna, and a dozen guest rooms, some with Jacuzzis and all wildly themed and loaded with loggish details; a trip to the website is suggested to handpick a vibe of choice. Next door is a 7,000-acre forest perfect for hiking and cross-country skiing. Some rooms share baths.

The Inn @ City Lights (1319 Mecklenburg Rd., 607/227-3003, www.theinnatcitylights.com, $135–155) offers warm service, roomy suites (some with full kitchen and woodstove), and cozy bedrooms, all with private bath and modern amenities. The garden is a nice place to relax or to enjoy Ithaca's fireworks displays on holidays.

The picturesque **William Henry Miller Inn** (303 N. Aurora St., 607/256-4553, www.millerinn.com, $155–185), an 1880 home and carriage house filled with stained glass and carved wood details, offers high-ceilinged rooms with private baths (some with Jacuzzis) and modern amenities, warm service, evening dessert with coffee, and gourmet breakfast with offerings such as Poached Eggs with Sun Dried Tomato Hollandaise or Crème Brulee French Toast.

For more bed-and-breakfast suggestions, contact the Ithaca/Tompkins County Convention & Visitors Bureau (904 E. Shore Dr., near Stewart Park, 607/272-1313 or 800/284-8422) or **Bed & Breakfast of Greater Ithaca** (800/806-4406, www.bbithaca.com). You can also check room availability by visiting the visitors bureau's website www.visitithaca.com.

FOOD

A number of casual eateries are located along Ithaca Commons. The 100 block of Aurora Street just off the Commons has one restaurant after another.

Famed worldwide for its best-selling cookbooks and natural foods, the cooperatively owned **◖ Moosewood** (215 N. Cayuga St., DeWitt Mall, 607/273-9610. $11) is a simple, casual place, crowded with rustic wooden tables. Named one of the 13 most influential restaurants of the 20th Century by *Bon Appetit* magazine, this creative vegetarian establishment continues to share its love of natural foods and produce. An outdoor dining area opens in the summer.

The upscale **Willow** (202 E. Falls St., 607/272-0656, $18) is a local favorite, serving contemporary American fare. Also serving contemporary American cuisine, as well as seafood, is the **Boatyard Grill** (525 Taughannock Blvd., 607/256-6228, $17), overlooking the waterfront.

Just a Taste Wine and Tapas Restaurant & Bar (16 N. Aurora St., 607/277-9463, average tapa $8) serves 50 wines by the glass and an international menu. Outside is a lovely garden. A couple blocks north, **Madeline's Restaurant and Bar** (N. Aurora and E. State Sts., on the Commons, 607/277-2253, $14) offers excellent Asian cuisine from a variety of countries. For the best Thai food in town, step into **The Thai Cuisine** (501 S. Meadow St., 607/273-2031, $12).

Hot spot **Maxie's Supper Club and Oyster Bar** (635 W. State St., 607/272-4136, $14), all done up in purples and reds, offers both spicy Cajun cuisine and stick-to-your-ribs Southern soul food. Everything's homemade at this family-run affair.

INFORMATION AND SERVICES

The **Ithaca/Tompkins County Convention & Visitors Bureau** (904 East Shore Dr., near Stewart Park, 607/272-1313 or 800/284-8422, www.visitithaca.com) is open 9 A.M.–6 P.M. Monday–Friday, 10 A.M.–4 P.M. Saturday, and 10 A.M.–4 P.M. Sunday mid-May–October, and 9 A.M.–5 P.M. Monday–Friday and 10 A.M.–5 P.M. Saturday November–mid-May.

In the Clinton House (116 N. Cayuga St., Ithaca Commons) is the **Ticket Center** (607/273-4497), which sells tickets for various arts organizations.

Seneca Lake

At 36 miles long and 618 feet deep, Seneca Lake is one of the deepest bodies of water in the United States. It seldom freezes over and is renowned for its superb lake-trout fishing. Given to sudden, capricious gusts of wind, it's the most mysterious of the Finger Lakes.

Ever since the days of the Native Americans, area residents have reported strange, dull rumblings coming from Seneca's depths. The sounds are usually heard at dusk in the late summer or early fall and are most distinct midway down the lake. The Native Americans believed that the rumblings were the voice of an angry god; early settlers considered them omens of disaster; science attributes them to the popping of natural gas released from rock rifts at the bottom of the lake.

Whatever the cause, the dull rumbles—a sound much like gunfire—may have had some portent, for during World War II, a huge munitions depot and naval station was built along Seneca's eastern shore. The naval station is now long gone, but the 11,000-acre Seneca Arms Depot remains. Officially, it functions to "maintain and demilitarize ammunition," but the herd of snow-white deer that roam the grounds can't help but make you wonder. The deer can best be seen from Route 96A at dawn and dusk.

At the northern end of Seneca Lake lies Geneva, a historic town whose South Main Street has been called "the most beautiful street in America." At the southern end is Watkins Glen, a rugged, 700-foot-deep gorge that's been turned into a natural theme park.

GENEVA

One of the larger towns in the region, Geneva is home to about 15,000 residents. Though overall a nondescript place, through its center runs the elegant South Main Street, lined with leafy trees, stately homes, and Hobart and William Smith Colleges.

Geneva was once a major Seneca settlement known as Kanadesaga. During the French and Indian War, the British erected a fort here from which they and the Seneca conducted murderous raids—only to be massacred themselves during the 1779 Sullivan campaign.

Soon after the Revolution, settlers began to arrive. A visionary land agent laid out the town along a broad Main Street and a public green. This gave the place an air of dignity which, during the 1800s, attracted an usually large number of retired ministers and spinsters. Geneva soon earned the nickname "The Saints' Retreat and Old Maids' Paradise."

In 1847, the Medical College of Geneva College (now Hobart) received an application of admission from one Elizabeth Blackwell of Philadelphia. The students and deans, assuming it to be a joke, laughingly voted to admit her. A few weeks later, to everyone's amazement, Ms. Blackwell arrived, and in 1849, she graduated—the first woman ever granted a medical diploma in America.

Prouty-Chew Museum

The only South Main Street mansion open to the public is the Prouty-Chew (543 S. Main St., 315/789-5151, 9:30 A.M.–4:30 P.M. Tues.–Fri., 1:30–4:30 P.M. Sat., free admission). Built in the Federal style in 1829 by a Geneva attorney, the house was enlarged several times in the 1850s and 1870s, which accounts for its eclectic look. Now home to the Geneva Historical Society, the museum showcases changing exhibits on local history and art.

Rose Hill Mansion

Three miles east of downtown lies Geneva's foremost visitor attraction—the fine 1839 Rose Hill Mansion (Rte. 96A, 315/789-3848, 10 A.M.–4 P.M. Mon.–Sat. and 1–5 P.M. Sun. May–Oct., adults $3, seniors and children 10–18 $2), built in the Greek Revival style with six Ionic columns out front. The mansion was once home to Robert Swan, an innovative farmer who installed the country's first large-scale drainage system. Tours of the house take visitors past a fine collection of Empire-style furnishings. Next door is the former carriage house; out front, an emerald green lawn slopes down to Seneca Lake.

Accommodations and Food

For dockside dining, try **Crow's Nest on Seneca Lake** (415 Boody's Hill Rd., off Rte. 96A near Rose Hill Mansion, 315/781-0600, $14). On the menu are sandwiches and salads, seafood and beef.

The extravagant, Romanesque **Belhurst Castle** (4069 Rte. 14 S., 315/781-0201, www.belhurst.com, $110–325 d, with breakfast) took 50 workers toiling six days a week four years to complete. Finished in 1889, it features everything from turrets to stained-glass windows. Inside is an upscale restaurant (average lunch entrée $9, average dinner entrée $24) serving continental fare for both lunch and dinner, and about a dozen modernized guest rooms that vary greatly in size and price. Out front are formal gardens and a lakefront beach. Also operated by Belhurst Castle is the lovely Georgian **Whitesprings Manor** and the brand new **Vinifera Inn**; the same contact information and rates apply.

The luxurious, all-suite **Geneva-on-the-Lake** (1001 Lochland Rd., 315/789-7190 or 800/343-6382, www.genevaonthelake.com, $210–550 d, with continental breakfast) is especially popular among honeymooners. The property centers on a 1911 mansion built in the style of a 16th-century Italian villa. Each suite differs from the next, and outside extend 10 acres of formal gardens. The dining room (average dinner entrée $25), open to the public for lunch and dinner, serves continental fare using fresh local produce.

DETOUR TO SODUS POINT AND ENVIRONS

Worth a 30-mile detour north of Geneva on Route 14 is Sodus Point, which overlooks Lake Ontario. The village boasts gorgeous views, an inviting public beach, and the handsome 1870 **Sodus Bay Lighthouse Museum** (7606 N. Ontario St., 315/483-

4936, 10 A.M.–5 P.M. Tues.–Sun. May–Oct., $3 adults, children 11–17 $1).

The real reason to venture up here, however, are the **Chimney Bluffs.** Located on the eastern side of Sodus Bay, the bluffs rise 150 feet above the lake like some giant confectionery delight. All pinnacles, spires, and peaks, they're part of a glacier-created drumlin that has been eroded, carved, and shaped by water, wind, and snow. Atop some of the pinnacles sit lone trees; below them extends a stony beach. Scuba divers exiting Lake Ontario are another unexpected sight on the beach.

Dozens of other drumlins (minus the pinnacles and peaks) can be found throughout this part of the Lake Ontario region. The only other places to view drumlins in North America are the areas bordering Lake Superior in Minnesota.

The Chimney Bluffs and its beach form part of the undeveloped Chimney Bluffs State Park. The park can be reached by taking Route 414 north to the end of Lake Bluff Road.

Alasa Farms

On your way to and from Sodus Point, you'll pass through serious farm country, heavy with rich black soil. Near the lake thrive apples, cherries, and peaches. Farther inland grow corn, wheat, potatoes, onion, and lettuce.

Off Route 14 just south of Sodus Point lies Alasa Farms (6450 Shaker Rd., Alton, 315/483-6321, June–Oct. by appointment). Once a 1,400-acre Shaker religious community, the site passed into private hands in the 1800s. Throughout the 1920s and 1930s, the farm raised everything from shorthorn cattle and hackney ponies to timberland and orchards, and today, it's still a 700-acre working farm. Visitors can opt for either a self-guided farm tour or an escorted tour of the Shaker Dwelling House.

Events

One of the region's foremost events is the **Sterling Renaissance Festival** (315/947-5783, www.sterlingfestival.com), held in Sterling, near Fair Haven, about 25 miles west of Sodus Point.

For seven weekends in July and August, the fest celebrates the Middle Ages with music, jousting, outdoor theater, crafts, and food.

SOUTH ON ROUTES 96A AND 414

From Rose Hill Mansion in Geneva, Route 96A heads south along the eastern shore of Seneca Lake. About 10 miles down is the 1,852-acre **Sampson State Park** (6096 Rte. 96A, 315/585-6392, parking $6–8), once a naval training station where thousands of soldiers trained during World War II. Today, the park is equipped with a marina, swimming beach, bathhouses, picnic area, playground, and 245-site campground. To reserve a campsite, call 800/456-CAMP.

South of Willard, Route 96A veers inland to Ovid, in the Cayuga Lake Area, where it hooks up with Route 414. Continue south on Route 414 to more small villages and a cluster of vineyards and wineries.

Wineries

Around the village of Lodi you'll find several wineries. Among them is the **Lamoreaux Landing Wine Cellars** (9224 Rte. 414, 607/582-6011, www.lamoreauxwine.com, 10 A.M.–5 P.M. Mon.–Sat., noon–5 P.M. Sun.) housed in a Greek Revival building with great views of the lake. Lamoreaux produces everything from chardonnay to pinot noir.

A few more miles down the road sprawls the highly commercialized **Wagner Vineyards** (9322 Rte. 414, 607/582-6450, www.wagnervineyards.com, 10 A.M.–5 P.M. Mon.–Sat., noon–5 P.M. Sun.), centered on a weathered octagonal building overlooking the lake. Established in 1979, Wagner produces over 75,000 gallons a year. On the premises is a microbrewery and **Ginny Lee Cafe** (607/582-6574), open for lunch and Sunday brunch only.

WINERIES SOUTH ON ROUTE 14

From Geneva, Route 14 heads south along the western shore of Seneca Lake past two excellent wineries. **Fox Run Vineyards** (670 Rte.

14, Penn Yan, 315/536-4616, www.foxrunvineyards.com, 10 A.M.–5 P.M. Mon.–Sat., noon–5 P.M. Sun.), is housed in an 1860s dairy barn with sweeping views of the lake. The **Anthony Road Wine Company** (1225 Anthony Rd., Penn Yan, 315/536-2182, www.anthonyroadwine.com, 10 A.M.–5 P.M. Mon.–Sat., noon–5 P.M. Sun.) is not particularly scenic but produces a good seyval and Riesling.

More good wineries cluster near the lake's southern end. Among them is the **Hermann J. Wiemer Vineyard** (3962 Rte. 14, Dundee, 607/243-7971, www.wiemer.com), run by a foremost viticulturalist. Born on the Mosel River in Germany, Wiemer is known for his Rieslings.

A few miles farther south is **Glenora Wine Cellars** (5435 Rte. 14, Dundee, 607/243-5511, www.glenora.com). Established in 1977, Glenora produces over 150,000 gallons a year and is best known for sparkling wines. The winery offers panoramic lake views and presents jazz concerts in summer.

Also on site is the large, modern, and very comfortable **Inn at Glenora Wine Cellars** (5435 Rte. 14, 607/243-9500, www.glenora.com, $160–255), which features big picture windows overlooking the vineyards and spacious guestrooms complete with private balconies or patios. Connected with the inn is an equally spacious restaurant (average entrée $17) and outdoor dining patio that serves tasty "regional fusion" specialties.

WATKINS GLEN AND VICINITY

At the southern tip of Seneca Lake lies Watkins Glen, named for the astonishing gorge that rips right through its center. Near the entrance to the glen, now a state park, stand family-style eateries and lots of souvenir shops.

Back in the 1950s and '60s, the main street of Watkins Glen and the steep roads surrounding it were the speedway of the American Grand Prix. During the races, as many as 75,000 spectators descended on the village, whose year-round population was—and is—under 3,000. Today, world-class auto races take place at the Watkins Glen International Race Track, four miles south of Watkins Glen.

There's a **Grand Prix Festival** (www.grand-prixfestival.com) in early September to commemorate the town's legacy. The 1948 American Grand Prix, complete with vintage cars, is reenacted in the streets of Watkins Glen.

Watkins Glen State Park

Created some 12,000 years ago during the last Ice Age, Watkins Glen (off Rte. 14/414, 607/535-4511, 8 A.M.–dusk daily May–Nov., parking $6–8) is a wild and raggedy gorge flanked by high cliffs and strange, sculpted rock formations. Through its center rushes Glen Creek, dropping some 700 feet in two miles over rapids, cascades, and 19 waterfalls.

Alongside the gorge runs the 1.5-mile Gorge Trail, made up of 832 stone steps, stone paths, and numerous bridges. The trail leads past tunnels, caves, and a natural stone bridge, all carved out of the sedimentary rock by Glen Creek. If you hike the trail on a fine summer's day, you'll have lots of company, but the gorge inspires awe nonetheless.

© SASCHA ZUGER
Watkins Glen State Park falls

The park also offers campgrounds; for reservations, call 800/456-CAMP.

Montour Falls

Route 14 leads south of Watkins Glen through narrow winding Pine Valley to Montour Falls, a small industrial community surrounded by seven glens. In the middle of town, flanked by buildings, is **Chequagua Falls,** plunging downward 165 feet into a deep pool. The falls are illuminated at night and near the top is a pedestrian bridge.

Along Genesee and Main Streets you'll find a handsome **National Historic District** composed of 24 brick buildings dating back to the 1850s. Among them is Memorial Library with Tiffany windows and the Greek Revival Village Hall.

Sports and Recreation

World-class auto racing takes place June–September at the **Watkins Glen International Race Track** (2790 County Rd. 16, off Rte. 14/414 S., 607/535-2481). Ticket prices depend on the race.

May–October, 50-minute cruises of Seneca Lake are offered every hour on the hour by **Captain Bill's Seneca Lake Cruises** (1 N. Franklin St., 607/535-4541). Captain Bill also runs dinner cruises.

Accommodations

One of the more idiosyncratic hostelries in the area is the **Seneca Lodge** (Rte. 329, off Rte. 14/414 at the south entrance to Watkins Glen State Park, 607/535-2014, $75–99). A favorite haunt of bow hunters and race mechanics, the lodge centers on a restaurant and Tavern whose back wall, bristled with arrows, looks like the hide of a porcupine and from whose ceiling hang Nascar Champs' tires and Formula One laurel wreaths. As the tradition goes, the first bow hunter to shoot a deer each season shoots an arrow into the wall. Accommodations consist of very basic camp-style A-frames, cabins, and motel rooms with one larger four bedroom available.

Magnolia Place Bed and Breakfast (5240

Rte. 414, Hector, 607/546-5338, www.mag-noliawelcome.com, $140–190), an 1830 farmhouse located about seven miles outside of Watkins Glen, offers eight suites overlooking Lake Seneca. Innkeepers talented in the culinary arts host wine tastings and create hot breakfasts of 'Dutch babies' with Cinnamon Biscuits, or corn fritters with house-smoked salmon, crème fraiche, and a poached egg, as well as providing homemade evening sweets and dinner or hors d'oeuvres on request.

Watkins Glen Harbor Hotel (16 N Franklin St., 607/535-6116, www.watkinsglenharborhotel.com, $159–229) situated right on the water is a lovely new hotel with an upscale boutique feel. A favorite of the NASCAR drivers and entourage during race weekends, the large airy rooms feature lush bedding and spa-style baths. Three dining options include al fresco in season, a classic country club sports bar, and Bluepointe Grille restaurant.

Food

Chef's Diner (Rte. 14, 607/535-9975) is a classic American eatery, now in its sixth decade. Come here for tasty pancakes or grilled-cheese sandwiches.

Wildflower Café and Crooked Rooster Brewpub (223-301 N. Franklin St., 607/535-9797, $8–14) offers tasty organic fare, from creative sandwiches to hearty meals. Bob and

June's Organic Coffee is roasted on the premises and Rooster Fish Fine Craft Ales are another big draw—ideal for tasting at $1.25 for 4-ounce samplers.

Chef-owned **Dano's Hueriger** (9564 Rte. 414, Lodi, 607/582-7555, $12) with glass-walled lakeside dining combines the tastes of a traditional Viennese wine restaurant with the Finger Lake's best vintages. Charcuterie and schnitzel, authentic Viennese casual ordering style and Austrian traditions, like a festival celebrating the harvest with newly fermented wine, add to the allure. A chef's table is available on request for parties of six or more.

Just west of the village, you'll find **Castel Grisch Estate** (3380 County Rd. 28, off Rte. 409, 607/535-9614, $8–16), a winery with a German-style restaurant. It's open for lunch and dinner Friday–Sunday. Outside is a deck with lake views.

At the Watkins Glen Harbor Hotel, **Bluepointe Grille** (16 N Franklin St., 607/535-6116, www.watkinsglenharborhotel.com, $26) is a fine dining restaurant where the talents of Chef Chris Hascall are expressed through signature dishes such as Rack of Lamb, Eggplant Strato, and Wild Mushroom Ravioli. Helping this success is the hotel's membership in the Finger Lakes Culinary Bounty, a program where properties sign on to use freshly delivered locally grown products in their menus.

Elmira

Elmira sits on both sides of the Chemung River, a few miles north of the Pennsylvania border. Some parts of the city are quite historic, with handsome stone and red-brick buildings; other parts are crumbling, windswept, and seriously depressed.

Once the site of a Seneca village, Elmira was first settled by whites in the 1780s. By the 1840s, the town was known for its lumbering and woolen mills, and by the 1860s, for its metal industries and iron furnaces. Elmira also served as a major transportation center,

sitting at the crossroads of the Erie Railroad, the Chemung River, and the Chemung and Junction Canals.

During the Civil War, the Union Army set up barracks in Elmira. In 1864, one of those barracks was turned into a prison camp for Confederate soldiers. The prison was poorly built and desperately overcrowded; thousands of prisoners died within a year.

Samuel Clemens, a.k.a. Mark Twain, spent more than 20 summers in Elmira. His wife, Olivia Langdon, grew up in the area and Twain

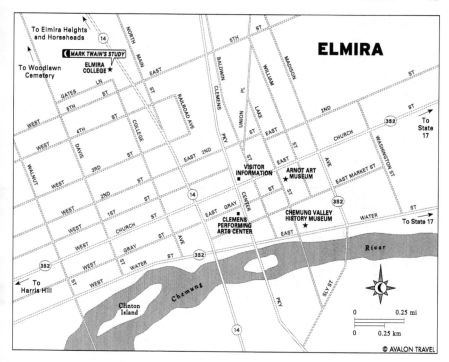

wrote many of his masterpieces—including *Tom Sawyer* and *The Adventures of Huckleberry Finn*—while staying at the Langdon family farm. Mark Twain's Study has since been moved onto the campus of Elmira College, which was one of the earliest colleges for women, founded in 1855.

Outside the city lies the National Soaring Center. Elmira has been known as the Soaring Capital of America ever since 1930, when the first National Soaring Contest took place here.

Most of Elmira is north of the Chemung River. Exiting off Route 17 onto Route 352W (Church St.) will take you into the heart of the city. Route 14N runs past Elmira College and Woodlawn Cemetery (off West Woodlawn Ave.).

In July and August, hour-long **trolley tours** (Chemung County Chamber of Commerce, 607/734-5137 or 800/627-5892) of Elmira's historical attractions are offered; call for details.

DOWNTOWN SIGHTS
◖ Mark Twain's Study

The story of Mark Twain and Olivia Langdon began in 1867 when Twain fell in love with her after viewing her portrait, shown to him by a friend as they were crossing the Atlantic. Upon arrival back in the United States, Twain immediately set up a meeting with Olivia. At first, she was not at all impressed. He was a rough-and-tumble self-made man; she was a refined young woman of a good family.

But Twain was stubborn. For the next two years, he visited Elmira regularly, and eventually won over the entire Langdon family. In fact, near the end of his courtship, Olivia—who was sickly and delicate—was only allowed to visit with him for five minutes a day because she became so excited.

Twain's former study (Park Pl., Elmira College Campus, 607/735-1941, www.elmira.edu, 9 A.M.–5 P.M. Mon.–Sat. June–Labor

Mark Twain's Study

Day, or by appointment, free admission), modeled after a Mississippi steamboat pilot house, was built for him by his sister-in-law. Twain once described it as "the loveliest study you ever saw. It is octagonal in shape with a peaked roof, each space filled with a spacious window and it sits perched in complete isolation on the very top of an elevation that commands leagues of valleys and city and retreating ranges of blue hill."

Inside, the study is simple and functional. A Remington Rand sits on a desk, a trunk inscribed with the name "Clemens" rests on the floor. His hat and pipe rest on a desk. Twain was one of the first writers to submit a typed manuscript to a publisher. A student guide is stationed at the study and offers details and stories about its history.

Woodlawn Cemetery

In Woodlawn Cemetery (1200 Walnut St., 607/732-0151, dawn–dusk daily), Samuel Clemens is buried in the Langdon family plot, along with his wife, his father-in-law, and his son-in-law Ossip Gabrilowitsch, a noted Russian-born pianist. A 12-foot-high monument commemorates the two famous men.

Adjacent to the main cemetery is the **Woodlawn National Cemetery** (1825 Davis St., 607/732-5411, dawn–dusk daily), containing the graves of the 2,963 Confederate soldiers who died in the Elmira prison. Surrounding the Confederate graves are the graves of 322 Union soldiers. When families came north to retrieve their loved ones, they saw what respect had been afforded the soldiers and many made the decision to leave them in their resting place.

Arnot Art Museum

In this restored 1833 neoclassical mansion (235 Lake St., at W. Gray St., 607/734-3697, www.arnotartmuseum.org, 10 A.M.–5 P.M. Tues.–Sat., 1–5 P.M. Sun., adults $5, seniors and students $4.50, children 6–12 $2.50) hangs a fine collection of 17th- to 19th-century European and 19th- to 20th-century American paintings. At the heart of the collection are works acquired by Matthias Arnot in the late 1800s. Among them are paintings by Breughel,

Daubigny, Rousseau, and Millet, hung floor to ceiling in the old salon style.

Behind the mansion, a handsome modern wing houses both temporary exhibitions and rotating selections from the museum's Asian, Egyptian, and pre-Columbian collections.

Chemung Valley History Museum

To learn more about Elmira'a past, stop into this local history museum (415 E. Water St., at Lake St., 607/734-4167, www.chemungvalleymuseum.org, 10 A.M.–5 P.M. Tues.–Sat., free admission). Featured are exhibits on the Seneca, Mark Twain in Elmira, and the Civil War prison camp.

NEARBY SIGHTS
◖ Harris Hill Soaring Center and National Soaring Museum

A few miles west of Elmira rises Harris Hill, an idyllic, woodsy spot surrounded by other hills and valleys that produce good updrafts. The Harris Hill Soaring Center (102 Soaring Hill Dr., off Rte. 352, 607/734-0641 or 607/796-2988, www.harrishillsoaring.org) has been attracting gliding and soaring aficionados since the 1910s.

Visitors to Harris Hill can take a glider ride aboard one of the delicate vessels parked in the airfield's hangar. This is truly one of the most unique experiences in the Finger Lakes and well, well worth a ride. Passengers' level of ease is considered as pilots tailor the ride to their comfort. All the pilots are FAA certified, and the rides take about 20 minutes, soaring from air current to air current high above the countryside. Sailplane rides are offered daily June–Labor Day, and weekends April–May and September–October; cost is $80 per person. Harris Hill also has a Juniors Organization in which teens may apply to learn to pilot a glider and receive FAA-certification.

Just down from the airfield sits the National Soaring Museum (51 Soaring Hill Dr., 607/734-3128, www.soaringmuseum.org, 10 A.M.–5 P.M. daily, adults $6.50, seniors $5.50, children 5–17 $4), a well designed museum which chronicles the history of Harris Hill and flying in America. Of special interest are the museum's 12 antique gliders and sailplanes, and the simulated cockpit.

National Warplane Museum

Run primarily by enthusiastic senior-citizen volunteers, this indoor-outdoor museum (17 Aviation Dr., Elmira-Corning Airport [Exit 51 off Rte. 17], 617/739-8200, www.warplane.org, 9 A.M.–5 P.M. Mon.–Sat., 11 A.M.–5 P.M. Sun., adults $7, seniors $5.50, children 6–17 $4, families $18) is dedicated to the restoration and maintenance of flying-condition WWII and Korean War aircraft. The planes are spread out like hulking insects all around a small visitors center and hangar where someone is always busy repairing something. A highlight of the museum's collection is the "Fuddy Duddy"—a B-17 Flying Fortress used during World War II.

One of the best times to visit the museum is during its Wings of Eagles Airshow, held the third weekend in August. Throughout the rest of the year, volunteers are always on hand to conduct personalized tours.

ACCOMMODATIONS AND CAMPING

A few miles south of Elmira lies the **Newtown Battlefield Reservation** (Lowman Rd. off Rte. 17, 607/732-6067) where Gen. John Sullivan won a decisive battle over a large force of Iroquois and Tories on August 19, 1779. Situated on a hilltop with wide-angled views of the Chemung Valley, the former battlefield is now a county park with hiking trails, a picnic area, and campgrounds.

Several miles north of downtown find the **Lindenwald Haus** (1526 Grand Central Ave., 607/733-8753, www.lindenwaldhaus.com $85–115), a romantic Italianate mansion built in 1875. Surrounded by five acres, the inn features 18 spacious guest rooms, long creaky hallways, and an airy living room that stretches most of the length of the house. Rocking chairs and braided rugs are everywhere. Some rooms share baths.

Elmira's Painted Lady Bed and Breakfast (520 W Water St., 607/846-3500,

Elmira's Painted Lady Bed and Breakfast

© SASCHA ZUGER

elmiraspaintedlady.com, $165–195) is located near the Westside Historic District. Guests can't help but leave this lovely and lovingly kept 1875 historic Victorian feeling like family, due to the warmth of the excellent innkeepers who manage that perfect level of constant at-the-ready service without being overpoweringly present or in the slightest way obtrusive. A truly stellar and generous hot breakfast, tailored to guests' taste, in-room fresh flowers, whirlpool soaking tubs, romantic fireplaces, the wide sitting porch, and 1880s billiard parlor where Samuel Clemens himself once puttered about, make this a can't miss spot. Modern amenities, flatscreen TVs with DVD, Wi-Fi, and spa robes add convenience to these Twain-themed suites.

FOOD

Charlie's Café and Bakery (205 Hoffman St., 607/734-1173) is back and a good choice for the downtown crowd, particularly for those with dietary restrictions.

Just out of town, **Sophie's Café** (485 Maple St., Big Flats, 607/562-2880) is a must stop for scone and pastry lovers. Try the Grape Pie in season—it's a regional delicacy. Combine pastries with tasty homemade soups, sandwiches, and salads (which come with a savory scone) for a great lunch. An extensive Hot Chocolate Bar, complete with homemade giant marshmallows and other accessories will put this café firmly in the hearts of anyone with a sweet tooth.

Third-generation **Hill Top Inn Restaurant** (171 Jerusalem Hill, 607/732-6728, $14) is just that and a friendly place to sit out on the large terrace and enjoy a gorgeous view of the valley below, just a stone's throw from the lookout where Clemens sat so inspired in his since-relocated study. The spot is popular with locals and large loads of tourists stopping in as a midway point between Niagara and NYC. Fortunately, the establishment has the space to accommodate. Generous portions of items like Haystack Crab and Ahi Sesame Lollipops and a good-sized $20 wine menu keep the crowd happy.

Corning

Strange though it might seem, Corning and its famed glass center is the third-most-popular tourist destination in New York State. Any surprise might be due to the misconception that visitors to the **Corning Museum of Glass** are in for a history lesson on the world's oldest baking pan rather than an extremely well designed museum dedicated to the art of decorative glass, with nary a Pyrex measuring cup in sight. Crowd control is down to a science here, so don't be put off by the sight of a tour bus or two in the parking lot.

Corning, current population 11,000, became a one-industry town not long after 1868, when the Flint Glass Company of Brooklyn relocated here. The company chose Corning largely because of its strategic position on the Chemung River and Chemung Canal, which would allow for the easy delivery of raw materials.

In 1875, the company began to produce specialized types of glass, such as railway signal lenses and thermometer tubing. In 1880, the lightbulb division was developed in response to Edison's invention, and by the early 1930s, Corning was manufacturing 1,250,000 bulbs a day. In 1915, the company's research and development department invented Pyrex. In the early 1970s, a fiber optics division was established.

Today, about 6,000 Chemung County residents still work for Corning, Inc. Many others are involved in the tourism industry, servicing visitors who come to town to visit the Corning Museum of Glass.

◖ CORNING MUSEUM OF GLASS

The state-of-the-art Glass Museum (1 Museum Way, Exit 46 off I-86, 607/937-5371 or 800/732-6845, www.cmog.org, 9 A.M.–5 P.M. daily, with extended hours to 8 P.M. in summer, adults $14, seniors $11.90, students $12.60, children under 20 free, discounted combo tickets with the Rockwell Museum of Western Art) sits surrounded by sleek corporate buildings on the north side of town. Its undulating walls are made of a blue-gray glass, while its modern entrance is built of four giant panes of glass.

The museum is divided into several sections, including the hands on Glass Innovation Center, which tells of scientific advances in glassmaking and allows guests to try their hand at exhibits showing different elements of the process, and the Glass Sculpture Gallery, the largest of its kind in the world. The heart of the institution, however, remains its main museum building, which showcases more than 10,000 glass objects at a time, many dramatically displayed in darkened rooms with spotlights. The oldest objects date back to 1400 B.C., the newest seen in famous designers' contributions to constantly changing installations. Among the many highlights are an iridescent vase from 10th-century Iran, an 11-foot-high Tiffany window, and a table-long glass boat cut by Baccarat in 1900.

With over forty daily shows (included in admission), such as the Hot Glass Show, Flameworking Demos, and a demonstration where visitors can whip up a drawing and see it created out of glass in front of their eyes by a master crafter, visitors can observe the art of glass up close. This is a far sight more fascinating than your typical 'historic glass blowing station' at a pioneer village setup. At the Steuben Factory, skilled craftspeople are at work. This is the only place in the world where Steuben glass is made.

As a non-profit, the massive gift shop is populated by the works of individual outside artisans, rather than any products made on site at the museum. Another option for a truly memorable souvenir would be to hit **The Studio.** Glassmaking classes for every age range from $10–25 and include an impressively sturdy and beautiful object to bring home (gorgeous ornaments created through glassblowing, colorful blooms on deceptively looking delicate twisted stems achieved through pulling the molten glass into flower petals in glassforming), each

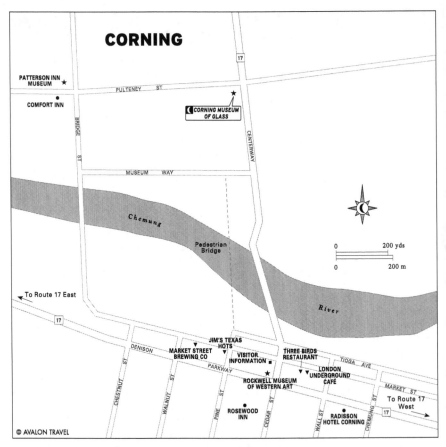

tailored to visitor's style and colors. This is a rewarding and unique artistic experience and very popular, so purchase tickets for designated time slots on entry to the museum.

HISTORIC MARKET STREET

After visiting the glass museum, most visitors stroll down a wide walkway that leads to Corning's historic downtown. This 19th-century district—once just another dying downtown—was extensively restored following Hurricane Agnes in 1972, when the street was all but destroyed by the flooding of the Chemung River.

Today, Market Street is brick sidewalks, locust trees, and one bustling shop or restaurant

after another. At one end are contemporary glass studios with artisans at work: **Vitrix Hot Glass Studio** 77 W. Market St., 607/936-8707, 9 A.M.–6 P.M. Mon.–Wed., 9 A.M.–8 P.M. Thurs.–Fri, 10 A.M.–8 P.M. Sat., noon–5 P.M. Sun.) and **Noslo Glass Studio** (89 W. Market St., 607/962-7886).

ROCKWELL MUSEUM OF WESTERN ART

Near the eastern end of Market Street presides the Rockwell Museum (111 Cedar St., 607/937-5386, www.rockwellmuseum.org, 9 A.M.–5 P.M. daily, with extended hours in summer, adults $6.50, seniors and students $5.50, children under

20 free, families $20, discounted combo tickets with the Corning Museum of Glass), which has nothing to do with Norman Rockwell and everything to do with Western art. Collected by Corning denizen Robert F. Rockwell, this is said to be the most comprehensive assemblage of Western art in the East.

The museum occupies the restored Old City Hall and is nicely arranged around three themes—the Indian, the Landscape, and the Cowboy. Works by Frederic Remington, Charles M. Russell, and Albert Bierstadt hang from the walls, and Navajo rugs drape the stairwell. Exhibit cases contain Native American art and artifacts.

After the crowds of the Corning Glass Center, the Rockwell Museum comes as a quiet relief. Rockwell was a passionate collector who once used the walls of his father's department store to exhibit his artwork, and the museum has an engaging, personal feel. The front desk provides families with scavenger hunts for particular items found within the artworks.

Enjoying the 'Music Margaritas and Sunsets on the Terrace' evenings on the terrace is a popular way to top off a tour, catch a live band, and soak in the fun atmosphere, on the rocks with salt. The museum also features **The Cantina Restaurant** (607/974-8226, www.974taco.com), a great place to grab a bite while in a southwestern sort of mood.

BENJAMIN PATTERSON INN MUSEUM COMPLEX

A half mile north of Market Street is a complex of restored historic buildings (59 W. Pulteney St., 607/937-5281, 10 A.M.–4 P.M. Mon.–Fri. Mar.–Dec., adults $3, children 6–18 $1) peopled by guides in costume dress. Buildings include the Benjamin Patterson Inn, complete with a women's parlor, tap room, and ballroom; the De Monstoy Cabin, furnished as it would have been by early settlers; and an 1860s barn equipped with antique farm implements.

ACCOMMODATIONS

Located near downtown is one of the area's most popular B&Bs, the handsome **Rosewood Inn**

(134 E. 1st St., 607/962-3253, www.rosewood-inn.com, $110–185). The five guest rooms and two suites are outfitted with antiques and have private baths. Downstairs is an elegant parlor with a fireplace, where afternoon tea is served.

Hillcrest Manor (Corner of 4th and Cedar Street, 607/936-4548, corninghillcrest-manor.com; $155–185 for fireplace suite) located in an 1890's Greek Revival mansion is a showplace for the area's art which first drew the owners to visit Corning.

FOOD

Visit **Jim's Texas Hots** (8 W. Market St., 607/936-1820) for ice cream and hot dogs, Texas-style. If grabbing a slice is more your style, try **Aniello's Pizzeria** (68 E. Market St., 607/962-2060) or **Atlas** (35 E. Market St, 607/962-2626) for brick oven style pizza, two of five pizza joints in town.

Locals hit rustic, family-run **Spencer's** (359 E. Market Ext., 607/936-9196), popular for their homemade sticky buns and breakfast menu with only one or two options over the $5 mark.

Tiny, hidden **Bento Ya Masako** (31 E Market Street, 607/936-3659) is tucked between two jewelry shops, up a flight of stairs, and marked only by a small 'Open' sign half-covering a Japanese symbol on a non-descript faded blue door. First timers might be caught off guard by the open kitchen at the top of the stairs in what looks like an apartment with two women cooking away. Just grab a seat at one of a handful of tables and prepare to be surprised. This cash-only establishment has limited hours (Tues.–Fri. lunch), but offers authentic Japanese and sushi to those in the know.

The **Market Street Brewing Co.** (63–65 W. Market St., 607/936-BEER) offers something for everyone, including rooftop and biergarten dining, dishes ranging from salads to steaks, a kids' menu, and, of course, fresh brews on tap; average entrée $15. The casually elegant **Three Birds Restaurant** (73 E. Market St., 607/936-8862) serves "progressive American fare" made with fresh local ingredients, and hosts a popular martini bar; average entrée $17; open for dinner only.

Keuka Lake

Gentle, Y-shaped Keuka Lake is the only one of the Finger Lakes with an irregular outline. The name means canoe landing in Iroquois, and the lake sports over 70 miles of curving lakeshore, scalloped with coves and bays.

At the southern head of Keuka Lake lies Hammondsport, site of the nation's first winery, established in 1860. The small-town Penn Yan occupies the lake's northern tip. Several Mennonite communities are scattered throughout the Keuka Lake region. Driving south between Penn Yan and Dundee along Routes 14A or 11, or north of Penn Yan along Routes 14A, 374, and 27, you're bound to pass a horse-and-buggy or two clip-clopping down the road. Handwritten signs advertising Mennonite quilts, furniture, or produce for sale sometimes appear by the roadside, while more permanent shops are located near Penn Yan and Dundee.

HAMMONDSPORT

Nestled between steep, verdant hills and Keuka Lake, Hammondsport is a fetching Victorian village with a lively tourist trade. At its center lies the Village Square, anchored by a big, white Presbyterian Church. Shops and restaurants line Shether Street, the main drag. Along the lakeshore are a sleepy park and two public beaches; the beach at the foot of Shether Street is said to be the best. However, local viticulture draws the most visitors. Tumbling down the surrounding hillsides are vineyard after vineyard, all supplying grapes for the area's nine wineries.

Glenn Hammond Curtiss, the pioneer aviator, was born in Hammondsport in 1878. Though not as well known as the Wright brothers, Curtiss made the world's first preannounced flight on July 4, 1908, when he piloted his "June Bug" airplane over 5,090 feet just outside Hammondsport. Curtiss developed the U.S. Navy's first amphibian airplane, opened the first flying school in America, and established the Curtiss Aeroplane Company—all in Hammondsport. During World War I,

the Curtiss company manufactured the popular Curtiss Jenny airplane, which later became a favorite of barnstormers.

Pleasant Valley Wine Company Visitor Center

Even if the thought of touring wineries bores you to tears, you might want to stop into this center (8260 Pleasant Valley Rd. [County Rd. 88], 607/569-6111, 10 A.M.–5 P.M. daily Apr.–Dec.; 10 A.M.–4 P.M. Tues.–Sat. Jan.–Mar., free admission), one of the largest tourist attractions in the region. The Pleasant Valley Wine Company is the oldest continuous maker of wine in the United States, founded by a group of Hammondsport businessmen in 1860.

The visitors center holds historic exhibits and an informative film, screened inside a 35,000-gallon former wine tank. A nearby working model train replicates the old Bath-Hammondsport Railroad, and a tasting bar offers products for sampling. Everything's very commercialized and the wine is mediocre, but the place is interesting nonetheless. Winery tours are offered throughout the day.

Bully Hill

One of the odder tales in the chronicles of viticulture is that of the battle waged over the name Taylor. Walter S. Taylor, a grandson of the founder of the Taylor Wine Co., was kicked out of the company in 1970 after publicly attacking its "incompetence, greed, and jealousy." Subsequently, he and his father Greyton began their own winery high on Bully Hill.

In 1977, Coca-Cola bought the Taylor Wine Co. and sued Walter for using his family name on his own labels. The case went to court and Walter lost, only to become a local hero. "They have my name and heritage but they didn't get my goat!" he proclaimed and flamboyantly struck out the Taylor name on all his labels. "Branded For Life, by a man that shall remain nameless without Heritage" reads the bylines in his brochures.

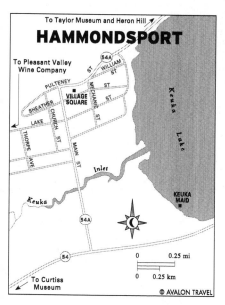

To Taylor Museum and Heron Hill ↗

HAMMONDSPORT

To Pleasant Valley
Wine Company

To Curtiss
Museum

0   0.25 mi
0   0.25 km

© AVALON TRAVEL

The **Wine and Grape Museum of Greyton H. Taylor** (8843 Taylor Memorial Dr., off Rte. 54A, 607/868-4814, 10 A.M.–5 P.M. Mon.–Sat. and Sun. noon–5 P.M. May–Oct., free admission) tells little of this story. Instead, it focuses on antique wine-making equipment and the delicate, lyrical Bully Hill labels, all drawn by "Walter St. Bully." Adjacent to the museum are the **Bully Hill Vineyards,** open for tastings. Also on site is the Bully Hill Restaurant, offering great views of the lake (see *Food,* below).

Other Wineries

One of the region's top wineries is **Dr. Frank's Vinifera Wine Cellars** (9749 Middle Rd., 607/868-4884, www.DrFrankWines.com). Dr. Frank, an immigrant from Ukraine who arrived in Hammondsport in 1962, was one of the first in the region to grow the European Vinifera grape. Today, his cellars, run by his son, are best known for their chardonnays and Rieslings.

A few miles beyond Bully Hill is the **Heron Hill Winery** (9301 Rte. 76, 607/868-4241, www.heronhill.com) offering chardonnays and Rieslings and more superb views of the

lake. Established in 1977, the 45-acre vineyard produces about 30,000 gallons of wine a year.

Both wineries are open 10 A.M.–5 P.M. Monday–Saturday and Sunday noon–5 P.M. May–October.

Glenn H. Curtiss Museum

The cavernous hangars of the former Curtiss Aeroplane Company now contain a sprawling museum (8419 Rte. 54, 607/569-2160, www.linkny.com/curtissmuseum, 9 A.M.–5 P.M. Mon.–Sat. and 11 A.M.–5 P.M. Sun. May–Oct., call for off-season hours, adults $7, seniors $5, students 7–18 $4) devoted to both Curtiss and the early history of aviation. About a dozen spiffy antique airplanes crowd the main hall, along with antique bicycles, motorcycles, propellers, and engines. Curtiss' first interest was the bicycle. One of his earliest planes, the Curtiss Pusher, looks just like a bike with double wings and wires attached.

A highlight of the museum is a replica of the famous "June Bug" airplane, built by volunteers in the mid-1970s. A Curtiss Jenny and delicate Curtiss Robin—resembling a giant grasshopper—stand nearby.

Recreation

The **Keuka Maid Dinner Boat** (607/569-2628, www.keukamaid.com), a 500-passenger vessel, offers lunch, brunch, and dinner tours May–October. The boat docks in the village off Route 54A; reservations are recommended.

Accommodations

The 30-room **Vinehurst Inn** (Rte. 54, 607/569-2300, $84 d, discounted weekly rates) features spacious motel rooms, many with cathedral ceilings, friendly service and included cont. breakfast. Some whirlpool suites and apartments available ($119–149).

Lake & Vine Bed and Breakfast (61 Lake Street, lakeandvinebb.info, 607/569-3282 $125–145), a newly remodeled 1868 Queen Anne style home offers four rooms, candlelit gourmet breakfast served with china and crystal and many modern amenities.

Elmcroft Manor Bed and Breakfast (8361

Pleasant Valley Road, 607/569-3071, www
.elmcroftmanor.com $200–300), an 1832 im-
pressive Greek Revival mansion with nicely
landscaped garden and grounds, features
upscale Italian-themed accommodations
stocked with quality amenities and com-
plimentary cheese and crackers, fruit juices
and sweets.

For a bit of novelty, 15 miles away in the village of Avoca is the storybook **C** **Caboose
Motel** (8620 Rte. 415, off Rte. 390, 607/566-
2216). Here, you can sleep in snug, restored 1916
train cabooses outfitted with all the modern con-
veniences and kept in trim shape ($85–90).

Food
In addition to its mouth-watering ice-cream
treats, the cozy **Crooked Lake Ice Cream
Parlor** (on the Village Square, 607/569-2751)
serves a good breakfast and lunch. Greenhouse
Cday. In the center of Bluff Point stands the
Garrett Memorial Chapel, a lovely Gothic-
style sanctuary built in memory of Charles
Garrett, the son of a wealthy winemaker, who
died of tuberculosis in his twenties. From Bluff
Point south, between Keuka's arms, runs the
eight-mile-long **Skyline Drive.**

PENN YAN
Named for its early Pennsylvanian and Yankee
settlers, Penn Yan is an attractive small town
(pop. 5,500), the seat of Yates County. Its downtown centers on historic Main Street, where
you'll find **Belknap Hill Books** (106 Main St.,
315/536-1186), packed with more than 20,000
out-of-print, used, and rare books.

On a windowless wall of **Birkett Mills**
(1 Main St.) are mounted half of an enormous griddle and the words: "The annual
Buckwheat Harvest Festival. Size of big
griddle used to make world record pancake,
Sept. 27, 1987. 28 feet, 1 inch." Birkett is the
world's largest producer of buckwheat products and maintains a small retail shop in its
offices (163 Main St., 315/536-3311).

Oliver House Museum
This local history museum (200 Main St.,
315/536-7318, 9:30 A.M.–4 P.M. Mon.–Fri.,
summer Sat. 10 A.M.–2 P.M., free admission),
housed in a handsome brick building, is run by
the Yates County Genealogical and Historical
Society. One especially interesting exhibit per-
tains to Jemima Wilkinson, the 18th-century
religious leader from Rhode Island who called
herself the "Publick Universal Friend."

Recreation
Auctions take place Saturday at 7 P.M. at **Hayes
Auction Barn** (1644 Rte. 14A, 315/536-8818).

The *Viking Spirit* **Cruise Ship** (680 East Lake
Rd., 315/536-7061, www.vikingresort.com) offers daily cruises May–October.

Accommodations
Near the downtown is the cozy **Fox Inn** (158
Main St., 315/536-3101 or 800/901-7997,
www.foxinnbandb.com, $155–180), a 1820s
Greek Revival home with five guest rooms and
formal gardens out back.

Situated on an 18-acre estate with great
views of both Keuka and Seneca Lakes presides **Merritt Hill Manor** (2756 Coates Rd.,
315/536-7682, www.merritthillmanor.com,
$169–189). The 1822 country manor offers
five guest rooms, a breezy porch, and a fire-
place-equipped living room.

Food
Diner aficionados will want to stop into the
squat, classic **Penn Yan Diner** (131 E. Elm St.,
off Main St., 315/536-6004), which dates back
to 1925. **Millers' Essenhaus** (1300 Rte. 14A,
Benton Center, 315/531-8260) is a Mennonite
restaurant serving such homemade specialties
as barbecue sandwiches, split pea soup, and
whoopie and shoofly pies.

Shopping
Midway between Penn Yan and Dundee
sprawls the **Windmill Farm and Market** (Rte.
14A, 315/536-3032, www.thewindmill.com),
the oldest and biggest of several indoor/out-
door farm-and-crafts markets operating in
the Finger Lakes. Every Saturday, May–
December, 8 A.M.–4:30 P.M., about 250 local

vendors set up shop in a large fairgrounds area off Route 14A. For sale are produce, flowers, furniture, crafts, wine, antiques, and homemade food. Many Mennonite families operate booths here.

In Dundee, you'll find **Martin's Kitchen** (4898 John Green Rd., 607/243-8197) selling homemade pickles, pickled watermelon rinds, jams, apple butter, and other Mennonite specialties.

Events

The **Yates County Fair** takes over the Penn Yan fairgrounds in mid-July. On the Fourth of July and the Saturday before Labor Day, the shores of Keuka Lake glow with magical **Rings of Fire,** as in the days of the Seneca. The Seneca lit bonfires to celebrate the harvest; today highway flares celebrate the holidays. For information about any of these events, call the Yates County Chamber of Commerce (315/536-3111).

Canandaigua Lake Area

The farthest west of the major Finger Lakes, Canandaigua is also the most commercialized. Rochester (pop. 235,000) is less than 30 miles away, and the lake has served as the city's summer playground since the late 1800s. At the northern end of the lake lies the historic city of Canandaigua, now largely a resort town. At the southern end rests the trim village of Naples.

Canandaigua is Iroquois for "The Chosen Place," and according to legend, the Seneca people were born at the south end of the lake, on South Hill. As the legend goes, the Creator caused the ground to open here, allowing the Seneca to climb out. All went well until a giant serpent coiled itself around the base of the hill. Driven by an insatiable hunger, the snake picked off the Seneca one by one until at last a young warrior slew him with a magic arrow. The dying serpent writhed down the hill, disgorging the heads of its victims as he went; large rounded stones resembling human skulls have been found in the area. South Hill is now part of the Hi Tor Wildlife Management Area.

Also connected with the Seneca is tiny Squaw Island, located in the northern end of the lake. The Seneca people relate that many women and children escaped slaughter by hiding out here during General Sullivan's 1779 campaign.

CANANDAIGUA

The sprawling city of Canandaigua has a wide and expansive feel. Through its center runs busy Main Street, a four-lane thoroughfare lined with leafy trees and imposing Greek Revival buildings set back from the street. At the foot of Main extends the lake and City Pier. Tourist-oriented businesses dominate.

Following the Revolution, two New Englanders, Oliver Phelps and Nathaniel Gorham, purchased what is now Canandaigua, along with the rest of western New York, from the Native Americans. The first white settlers arrived in 1789, and shortly thereafter, the first land office in the United States was established near present-day Main Street.

On November 11, 1794, the Seneca chiefs and Gen. Timothy Pickering met in Canandaigua to sign what was later known as the Pickering Treaty. A document of enormous significance, the treaty granted whites the right to settle the Great Lakes Basin. An original copy of the treaty can be found in the Ontario County Historical Society Museum.

Sonnenberg Gardens and Mansion

In the heart of the bustling downtown sits a serene 50-acre garden estate (151 Charlotte St., 585/394-4922, www.sonnenberg.org, 9:30 A.M.–5:30 P.M. daily June-Oct., adults $10, seniors $9, students $5, children under 12 free), composed of nine formal gardens, an arboretum, a *long* turn-of-the-20th-century greenhouse, and a massive 1887 stone mansion. The Smithsonian Institution credited the place "one

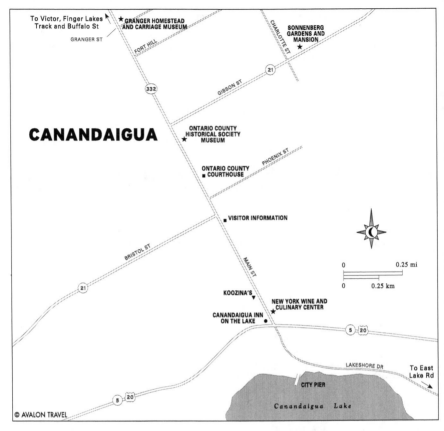

of the most magnificent late-Victorian gardens ever created in America."

Sonnenberg (German for "Sunny Hill") was once the summer home of Mary Clark and Frederick Ferris Thompson. Mr. Thompson, whose father helped to establish the Chase Bank, was co-founder of the First National City Bank of New York City.

The estate's nine gardens were created by Mrs. Thompson as a memorial after her husband's death in 1899. A classic Rose Garden features over 4,000 rose bushes, and the Japanese Garden took seven workers six months to create. The secluded Sub Rosa Garden contains statues of Zeus, Diana, and Apollo. The Blue & White Garden contains only blue and white flowers.

Visitors to Sonnenberg can wander freely—even the mansion is self-guided-though guided walking tours are also offered June–September. Near the entrance is an inviting café, housed in one of the greenhouses, and the huge, commercial **Finger Lakes Wine Center** (585/394-9016, 11 A.M.–4:30 P.M. daily, May–Oct.), selling regional wines.

Granger Homestead and Carriage Museum

This 1816 Federal-style mansion (295 N. Main St., 585/394-1472, www.grangerhomestead.org, 1–5 P.M. Tues.–Sun. May–Oct., adults $6, seniors $5, students $2) once housed Gideon Granger, U.S. postmaster general

Sonnenberg Gardens

under Presidents Jefferson and Madison. The home—"unrivalled in all the nation," Granger once boasted—is especially notable for its elaborate carved moldings and mantelpieces, and for its fine original furnishings.

Dark, towering trees surround the house. Out back is a carriage museum, packed with about 50 spit-and-polish coaches, sporting carriages, sleighs, commercial wagons, and an undertaker's hearse.

Ontario County Historical Society Museum

To learn more about the history of Canandaigua, step into this local museum (55 N. Main St., 585/394-4975, 10 A.M.–4:30 P.M. Tues.–Fr., 11 A.M.–3 P.M. Sat., admission $2), situated in a handsome brick building. On display is the original Six Nations' copy of the Pickering Treaty with the signatures of the Iroquois leaders Red Jacket, Cornplanter, Handsome Lake, Farmer's Brother, Little Beard, and Fish Carrier. Each signed with an X. The museum also features "life masks" of Abraham Lincoln (plaster-of-Paris masks taken

from a mold of his face), a small children's discovery area, and temporary exhibits.

Ontario County Courthouse

Dominating downtown Canandaigua, and indeed much of the surrounding countryside, is the bulbous dome of the Ontario County Courthouse (27 N. Main St., at Gorham, 585-396-4200, 8:30 A.M.–5 P.M. Mon.–Fri.). Hung in the two courtrooms of this 1858 Greek Revival structure is a marvelous collection of portraits. Among them are likenesses of Red Jacket and Susan B. Anthony, who was tried here in 1873 for voting in the national election in Rochester. She was found guilty and fined $100. A boulder on the courthouse grounds commemorates the Pickering Treaty, signed here in 1794.

Recreation

The *Canandaigua Lady* (205 Lakeshore Dr., 585/396-7350) is a 150-passenger paddlewheel boat offering lunch, dinner, and moonlight cruises May–October. **Captain Gray's Boat Tours** (5 Main St., 585/394-5270) features one-hour narrated tours of the lake daily July–August, weekends May–October; the boat leaves from behind the Canandaigua Inn on the Lake.

Seven miles northwest of Canandaigua lies **Finger Lakes Gaming & Race Track** (Rtes. 332 and 96, Exit 44 off I-90, 585/924-3232). Thoroughbred racing takes place Friday–Tuesday April–November. Also on site are 1,000 video-gaming machines.

Accommodations

The Canandaigua region is home to many luxury B&Bs. One of the best is the snug, 1795 Colonial **(** **Acorn Inn** (4508 Rte. 64 S, Bristol Center, 585/229-2834, www.acorn-innbb.com, $165–240 d), which has achieved the AAA four diamond rating for nine years, a rarity for a B&B. Once a stagecoach stop, the inn now pampers guests with comfy canopy beds, luxurious private baths, an outdoor hot tub, and multicourse breakfasts.

On the waterfront stands the **The Inn on the Lake** (770 S. Main St., 585/394-7800 or 800/228-2801, www.theinnonthelake.com, $174–255), a full-service hotel and conference center. Among its features are 147 nicely appointed guest rooms, many with patios or balconies; a pristine outdoor pool; saunas; and the airy, inviting Nicole's restaurant (see *Food*, below). The restaurant looks out to the lake and the tiny (un-PC-like-named) Squaw Island. At only 20 by 50 yards, the wild tree-covered spot where Native Americans were said to have placed their women and children for safety during skirmishes can be reached by kayak (**Canandaigua Sailboarding** (585) 394-8150, $12 hr.).

Not too far away is the plush 1810 **Morgan-Samuels B&B Inn** (2920 Smith Rd., 585/394-9232, www.morgansamuelsinn.com, $180–265), which offers six guest rooms, eight fireplaces, tennis courts, and gourmet breakfasts by candlelight. High on a bluff overlooking Deep Run Cove stands the peaceful turn-of-the-century **Thendara Inn** (4356 E. Lake Rd., 585/394-4868, $185–270 d), containing four spacious guest rooms furnished with antiques and a good restaurant.

Entertainment

During the summer, the Rochester Philharmonic Orchestra performs every weekend at the **Finger Lakes Performing Arts Center** (Rte. 364 and Lincoln Hill Rd., 585/325-7760), an outdoor amphitheater. Rock, jazz, and pop-music concerts are sometimes presented as well.

New York Wine and Culinary Center

(800 South Main St., 585/394-7070, www.nywcc.com) A treat for foodies, this beautiful 20,000sq ft facility houses a tempting gift shop with unique trinkets for culinary minded visitors, an exhibit room dedicated to the history of New York's culinary, wine and agriculture industries trimmed in wood reclaimed from century-old redwood wine barrels, glass-walled educational theatre where classes and demos in progress can be observed and the occasional food show program is filmed, an impressive **Tasting Center** featuring the state's finest wines and beers in a warm wood and stone setting and **The Taste of New York Restaurant,** where locally farmed ingredients come together in excellent meals with suggested wine and beer pairings to bring out the fullest flavors of the food.

Live music makes weekend evenings a great time to visit for beer lovers as a rotating selection of eleven brews, chosen from New York's 60 craft breweries, are featured on tap (flight tasting available), as well as 20 bottle choices from the state. New York State Charcuterie Sampler and Artisan Cheese Plate are two good choices for sipside nibbling.

Food

Koozina's (699 S. Main St., 585/396-0360) is a lively spot specializing in wood-fired pizza and pasta dishes; average entrée $9.

Nicole's at the Inn on the Lake (770 S. Main St., 585/394-7800) offers great views of the lake and contemporary American fare. It's open for breakfast, lunch, and dinner; average dinner entrée $18.

The Victorian **Thendara Inn** (4356 E. Lake Rd., 585/394-4868) serves American cuisine in three period dining rooms with panoramic views of the lake; in summer, an outdoor patio is opened up (average entrée $18; open for dinner only). Also at the inn is the more casual **Boathouse,** serving lighter fare for both lunch and dinner.

VICTOR

About 10 miles northwest of Canandaigua sprawls the village of Victor, worth visiting because of the **Ganondagan State Historic Site** (1488 Victor-Bloomfield Rd., 585/742-1690, www.ganandagan.org, 9 A.M.–5 P.M. Tues.–Sun. May–Oct., adults $3, children $2). During the 17th century, atop this grassy lime-green knoll, stood an important Seneca village and palisaded granary. The village was home to about 4,500 people; the granary stored hundreds of thousands of bushels of corn. All was destroyed in 1687 by a French army led by the governor of Canada. The French wished to eliminate the Seneca as competitors in the fur trade.

A visit to Ganondagan, which means "Town of Peace," begins with an interesting video that tells the story of the Seneca Nation and that of Jikohnsaseh, or Mother of Nations. Together with "The Peacemaker" and Hiawatha, Jikohnsaseh was instrumental in forging the Five Nations Confederacy; it was she who proposed that the Onondangan chief, who at first refused to join the confederacy, be appointed chairman of the Chiefs' Council. Jikohnsaseh once lived in the vicinity of Ganondagan and is believed to be buried nearby. No one searches for her grave, however, as a sign of respect.

Outside the visitors center begin three trails that lead over gentle terrain past informative plaques. The Trail of Peace relates important moments in Seneca history. The Earth of Our Mother Trail identifies plants important to the Seneca. The Granary Trail re-creates the day in 1687 Ganondagan was destroyed, through journal entries from the French forces.

To reach the site, from Rte. 332 heading north, turn left onto County Road 41 to Victor-Bloomfield Road. Trails stay open year-round 8 A.M.–sunset.

PALMYRA

About 15 miles due north of Canandaigua is Palmyra, an old Erie Canal town where Joseph Smith allegedly received, from the angel Moroni, a set of gold tablets inscribed with the Book of Mormon. The Hill Cumorah Pageant, the largest outdoor pageant in the United States, celebrates that event every July.

Downtown Palmyra is small and compact, lined with sturdy brick buildings. At each corner of the intersection of Main Street and Route 21 stand four soaring churches—a fact that once made it into *Ripley's Believe It or Not.* Just west of downtown is a graceful stone **Erie Canal Aqueduct,** off Route 31.

In downtown Palmyra are three small museums run by Historic Palmyra. On the outskirts of town are the Hill Cumorah Visitor Center and Joseph Smith Farm, run by the Mormon Church.

Historic Palmyra

The **William Phelps General Store** (140 Market St., 315/597-6981) was operated by the Phelps family from the 1860s until the 1940s. The museum recreates the general store of the 1890s and is an incredible untouched place to poke around, with excellent guides leading the way back into a simpler time.

The **Alling Coverlet Museum** (122 Williams St., off Main, 315/597-6737 or

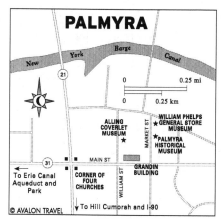

© SASCHA ZUGER

Phelps General Store is a re-creation of an 1860s family-run store.

315/597-6981) houses the largest collection of handwoven coverlets in the United States. Often referred to as the American tapestry, coverlets are ornate bed coverings made out of wool, cotton, or linen.

The nearby **Palmyra Historical Museum** (132 Market St., 315/597-6981) occupies the former St. James Hotel. Exhibits here include 19th-century furniture, Erie Canal art and artifacts, children's toys, stern Victorian portraits and a tour led by an expressive guide who brings the historic objects to life with animated anecdotes.

Finally, All three museums are open 1–4 p.m. Tuesday–Saturday June–September. Admission is free.

Hill Cumorah Visitor Center

A good place to learn about the Mormon religion is this modern center (603 Rte. 21, 315/597-5851, www.hillcumorah.com, 9 a.m.–5 p.m. Mon.–Sat., 1–5 p.m. Sun., with extended hours in summer, free admission), four miles south of the downtown. Most visitors are well-scrubbed Mormons straight from the heartland, but nonbelievers are welcome and are left more or less in peace to peruse the exhibits. A film provides a good introduction to Mormon history and beliefs, and exhibits tout the growth of the religion. There are currently about nine million Mormons worldwide, though only 1,500 live in upstate New York.

Behind the center stands Hill Cumorah, the drumlin where Joseph Smith is said to have found the gold tablets on September 22, 1827. It took him years to translate the tablets, and after he was done, he reburied them. Atop Hill Cumorah today is a gold statue of the angel Moroni.

Joseph Smith Farm and Sacred Grove

Born in Vermont in 1805, Joseph Smith first came to Palmyra with his family in 1815. The Smiths were farmers, and Joseph—described by one contemporary as a "quiet, low-speaking, unlaughing" boy—lived in this simple, white clapboard house (29 Stafford Rd., 315/597-4383 or 315/597-5851, 9 a.m.–5 p.m. Mon.–Sat., 1–5 p.m. Sun., free admission) until he was 22. He received his first vision in the Sacred Grove behind the house when he was only 14.

SOUTH ON ROUTES 364 AND 245

Heading south down Canandaigua's eastern shore, you'll pass through a series of picturesque valleys. At the southern end of the lake, the route skirts around South Hill and the **High Tor Wildlife Management Area** (585/226-2466). Hiking trails traverse the preserve, which is also one of the few places left in New York where you can still spot bluebirds—the state bird. The main entrance to the area is off Route 245 between Middlesex and Naples.

NAPLES

Just south of Canandaigua Lake, surrounded by hills, lies Naples, population 2,500. A tidy village with a brisk tourist trade, Naples centers around a historic **Old Town Square.** Naples is one of the best places in the Finger Lakes to sample a sweet regional specialty—**grape pie.** The pies, made with dark grapes, are only available during the harvest season in fall.

Widmer Wine Cellars

One mile due north of the Old Town Square is Widmer's (1 Lake Niagara Ln., off Rte. 21, 585/374-6311, www.widmerwine.com, noon–4:00 P.M. daily May–Dec., free admission)—one of the largest, oldest, and most commercialized wineries in the region. Tours start in a cool stone cellar filled with enormous oak vats, and end in a busy bottling plant that processes 300,000 cases of wine a year.

Widmer's has been producing Manischewitz, a kosher wine, since 1986. The wine is made in a separate winery equipped with all-stainless-steel vats. Rabbis come down from Rochester to oversee the process.

Cumming Nature Center

About eight miles northwest of the village lies the 900-acre Cumming Nature Center (6472 Gulick Rd., 585/374-6160, 9 A.M.–4:30 P.M. Sat.–Sun., admission $3), owned by the Rochester Museum and Science Center. A veritable outdoor museum, the preserve holds six miles of themed trails leading through forests and wetlands. The Conservation Trail illustrates theories of forest management; the Pioneer Trail, complete with a reconstructed homestead, teaches about the early settlers' lives. The Beaver Trail focuses on the principles of ecology, and the Iroquois Trail focuses on Native American life. Near the entrance is a visitors center.

Gannett Hill

Scenic Route 21 heads due north out of Naples to the highest point in Ontario County—Gannett Hill, 2,256 feet above sea level. Now part of Ontario County Park, the hill offers bird's-eye views of the surrounding countryside.

Food

Bob and Ruth's (204 Main St., Old Town Square, 585/374-5122) is a village institution containing both a casual dining area and the more formal Vineyard Room. Specialties range from rotisserie chicken to Angus beef (average entrée $17). In summer, an outdoor patio opens up.

The historic 1895 **Naples Hotel Restaurant** (111 S. Main St., 585/374-5630) specializes in traditional American fare; on Saturdays, live music is often presented in the hotel's rathskeller downstairs (average entrée $14). Five rooms are also available here for overnight guests ($75–125 d).

The Little Finger Lakes and Beyond

LITTLE FINGER LAKES

West of the six major Finger Lakes extend what are known as the little Finger Lakes: Honeoye (pronounced Honey-oy), Canadice, Hemlock, and Conesus. Honeoye sports a village of the same name at its northern end, and Conesus—closest to Rochester—is crowded with summer homes. Canadice and Hemlock serve as reservoirs for Rochester and remain largely undeveloped. Set in deep, wooded valleys with no towns nearby, these are also the highest of the Finger Lakes—1,100 and 905 feet respectively.

At the southwestern end of Honeoye lies the largely undeveloped **Harriet Hollister Spenser State Park** (Canadice Hill Rd. [Rte. 37], 585/335-8111). Set on Canadice Hill, the park offers great views of the lake and—on a clear day—the Rochester skyline.

Another quirky stop outside Honeoye is the unusual **Wizard of Clay** (7851 Rt 20A, Bloomfield, 585-229-2980 www.wizardofclay.com), where the Kozlowski potters use 100,000 pounds of clay each year hand-throwing the family's functional creations. The workshop is open to tour and see each stage of the process, even that of his unique patented Bristoleaf collection, made by pressing locally collected leaves into the soft clay before firing, leaving the imprints to be glazed for a final vase or picture frame. A densely pinned map on the wall shows the hometowns of thousands of visitors.

LETCHWORTH STATE PARK

Along the Genesee River at the far western edge of the Finger Lakes plunges one of the most magnificent sights in the state: the 17-mile-long **Letchworth Gorge,** now part of a state park (off Rtes. 36 and 19A, Castile, 585/493-3600, 6 A.M.–11 P.M. daily, $6–8 for parking). Dubbed the "Grand Canyon of the East," the gorge is flanked by dark gray cliffs rising nearly 600 feet. All around grows a dense, thicketed forest;

NUNDA/LETCHWORTH

A stay at Oakhill Farm Bed and Breakfast will provide a beautiful farm experience.

© SASCHA ZUGER

Genesee River flowing through Letchworth State Park

through the center of things sparkle three thundering waterfalls. Excellent hiking and snowshoeing are available through the wild terrain.

Much of the Letchworth Gorge was purchased by industrialist William P. Letchworth in 1859. A conservationist and humanitarian, Letchworth bought the gorge both for his own personal use and to save the falls from becoming Rochester's hydroelectric plant. Before his death in 1910, he deeded the gorge to the people of New York to be used as a permanent park.

One main road runs through the park alongside the gorge, affording scenic views. At the southern end stand the Glen Iris Inn, a favorite luncheon spot, and the Letchworth Museum. Recreational facilities include 20 hiking trails ranging from one-half to seven miles in length, two swimming pools, 82 cabins, and a 270-site campground.

The park can be entered from Mt. Morris (off Rte. 36), Portageville (off Rtes. 19A or 436), or Castile (off Rte. 19A); the Portageville entrances are closed in winter. For camping reservations, call 800/456-CAMP.

LETCHWORTH MUSEUM

Across from the Glen Iris Inn is a rambling museum (585/493-2760, 10 A.M.–5 P.M. daily May–Oct.) haphazardly packed with exhibits on the Seneca, William Letchworth, and the gorge's natural history. Note especially the exhibits relating to Mary Jemison, the "white woman of the Genesee."

The daughter of Irish immigrants, Jemison was taken prisoner by the Seneca at the age of 15 and lived the rest of her life among them. She married first a Delaware warrior and then, following his death, a Seneca chief; she bore seven children, and became a Seneca leader in her own right. Under the Big Tree Treaty of 1797, she was granted close to 18,000 acres along the Genesee River. Eventually, however, Jemison was moved to the Buffalo Creek Reservation with the rest of her people, where she died at the age of 91.

Letchworth moved Jemison's remains to the gorge in 1910 when her grave was in danger of being destroyed, and today, the **Mary Jemison Grave** stands on a hill behind the museum. Also on the hill is the **Council House** in

one of the three Genesee River falls at Letchworth State Park

which the last Iroquois council on the Genesee River was held on October 1, 1872. In attendance were the grandchildren of Red Jacket, Joseph Brant, and Mary Jemison; and William Letchworth and Millard Fillmore.

ACCOMMODATIONS
Glen Iris Inn

The stately, yellow-and-white **❮ Glen Iris Inn** (585/493-2622, www.glenirisinn.com, $95–120) sits in a large flat field overlooking the 107-foot Mid Falls. Once the home of William Letchworth, the Victorian mansion is now a modernized inn with 15 comfortable guest rooms, a library with a good collection of regional books, and a gift shop. The inn's bustling restaurant, flanked by picture windows, specializes in gourmet salads prepared tableside, seafood, and veal; open for breakfast, lunch, and dinner; average dinner entrée $18.

For a serene, scenic splurge, check availability for the signature **Cherry Suite at the Glen Iris Inn** room ($210) which features patterned hardwood floors, a whirlpool tub and a balcony overlooking the incredible middle falls. Guests of this room reclining on the balcony make all passing visitors jealous with their perch above

the glass-walled restaurant. Four bedroom **The Stone House** ($350 for up to 8pp) is another option rented by Letchworth State Park, situated across from Inspiration Point overlook.

Oakhill Farm Bed and Breakfast

This area is beautifully rural, which includes a lack of accommodation other than a chain hotel or two. One other gem situated near the far entrance to the park is Oakhill Farm Bed and Breakfast (8983 Oakland Road, Nunda, 585/468-5441, www.OakhillFarmNY.com, $139). If you're lucky enough to secure their only room, you will not be disappointed. Private entrance to the modernly appointed room, bath, full eat-in kitchen stocked with a gift basket of local favorites and homemade coffeecake, large garden and fountain view windows and balcony overlooking horse pastures and rolling hills add to this special property. Meticulously kept, endless fences lead to a swimming and fishing pond, complete with tiny imported sand beach, romantic sunset and stargazing historic carriage rides (pulled by the owner on a sparkling tractor), hiking and riding trails add up to an idyllic farm experience. Horseowners, take note, boarding is available in the large spotless barn, $15 per horse.